FOOD THAT WORKS

**REAL MEALS TO
SURVIVE THE 9 TO 5**

MALIA DELL

foodthatworks.info

Notice

This book is for educational purposes only. The ideas and suggestions in this book were designed to help you make informed decisions about your health. This book is not intended as a substitute for medical advice. Neither the author nor the publisher is responsible for any adverse effects due to the use of the information contained in this book.

Mention of specific companies or brand names in this book does not imply that they endorse this book.

ISBN-13: 978-0-9963950-6-9 (softcover)
ISBN-13: 978-0-9963950-0-7 (eBook)
First Edition

Edited by Paula Jacobson & Sheilah Kaufman of Cookbook Construction Crew

Cover design by Camden Design

Book design by Camden Design

Food Photography by Dave Clough, pages 36, 53, 58, 61, 63, 66, 81, 83, 85, 88, 89, 107, 127, and 134.

Food Styling by Ben Curtis, Malia Dell & Tim English

Photography by Jacinda Martinez, Kristin Kipp, Malia Dell, Nicole Marie Fuller & Suzanne Rea

Author Photograph by Katherine Wetherbee

Illustrations by Malia Dell

Dedication

This book is dedicated to our lifelong
journey of finding new and improved ways
to nourish ourselves with food, laughter,
and love. Practice makes practice!

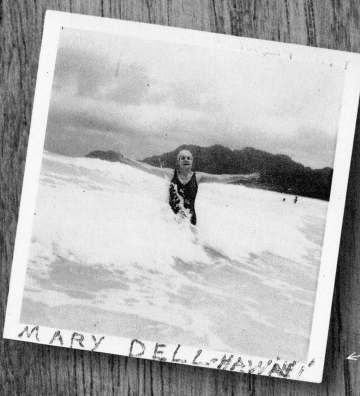

MARY DELL-HAWAII

This photo was taken
on my Grandma's first
trip to Hawaii. It
reminds me to try new
things and laugh!

CONTENTS

FOREWORD

By Mellisa Kelly

I'VE HAPPILY KNOWN Malia for several years now, ever since she came to work at my restaurant, Primo. Bright-eyed and inquisitive, Malia was extremely excited about food techniques, quality, and healthy living. She became famous for always coming to work with a stuffed Tupperware container or a small meal in a jar!

I love how, with this book, she makes easy tasks of planning, shopping, and cooking. Her intuitive guide includes building a restaurant-like pantry, making sure a supply of healthy choices are always on hand, and making quick and easy recipes that are not only tasty but nutritious as well. Another stellar idea Malia stresses is the importance of not wasting food, which is a vital skill in the kitchen. Her casual style and sense of humor make it easy to pick up this book and get started. It is well thought out and beautifully executed. Malia's personality saturates each page.

Being organized in the kitchen and cooking the way Malia recommends will not only save you money but will also keep you healthy and engaged in life, family and friends.

Watching Malia work hard and follow her dream has been an inspiration. This will be a frequently used cookbook—the pages tattered and stained.

This book is real. Read it. Relish it. Live it, and be healthy!

Melissa Kelly is the Owner and Executive Chef of Primo Restaurant in Rockland, Maine. She is the 1999 and 2013 recipient of the James Beard Award: Best Chef in the Northeast, making her the first two-time winner of this prestigious award. Recently, she was recognized in Forbes as one of the top ten female chefs in the nation.

AUTHOR PREFACE

At twenty-three I took the leap of my life, I began to cook.

I WAS BORN in Honolulu and lived there for the first six years of my life. My parents were sort of nomads; we moved to Chicago, then Vermont, and Massachusetts. Due to their interests in learning about different cultures and customs, my parents' love for art, travel, and new experiences extended into everything we did. Growing up in these diverse cities and states I was exposed to a variety of ethnic foods.

So you'd think I'd know a thing or two about eating well. The truth is I did not learn to cook until I was twenty-three years old, so up to that point, my chosen diet revolved around frozen pizza bites and drive-thru windows. Then I finally had my "Aha!" moment and hit food puberty, which I like to call, "fooburty," and I learned to cook. Once I realized how amazing I felt when I started eating fresh food, I never looked back.

The idea for this book was born from my abhorrence of the corporate office lunch culture, which pressured me into settling for mostly packaged or canned foods that were pulled out of a bag, yanked from a desk drawer, or grabbed from a shelf, and then microwaved, day in and day out. I saw the effects it was having on me and every single one of my coworkers.

I believed that there *had* to be a way to balance the demands of the 9 to 5 work schedule with home-cooked meals. I came to the conclusion that organized shopping lists, chopped vegetables, and quick recipes requiring minimal cleanup were essential to making homemade meals possible every day throughout the workweek. I began packing my "Purse Kitchen" and bringing my own food everywhere I went; this ignited curiosity in the people around me. It was undeniable that there was a demand for access to simple clean food, and there was also a deep sense of interest and urgency from hard-working hungry people. They wanted to eat better and get back to basics. All they needed was a simple plan and a Type A person to create it, like me.

With a degree in sociology and a lust for travel in my blood, I left the corporate world of Boston in 2011 to live in the Mediterranean countries of Spain and Turkey. I observed how other cultures managed their diets and kitchens. I quickly realized a commonality in their daily meals: they were made with fresh ingredients and always prepared in the home. The dishes themselves were simple. They were homemade with the best fresh ingredients. They were divine!

Upon returning to the states, I put my backpack down in Rockland, Maine, so I could write this cookbook. My food journey continued as I worked at one of the most prestigious restaurants in America, Primo. I was inspired daily as I learned from two-time, James-Beard-Award-winning Chef Melissa Kelly how to utilize crossover ingredients, strategically use up every morsel, and run an efficient kitchen with minimum waste. And yes, she taught me how to slaughter chickens, turkeys, and rabbits. It was pretty badass!

I am not a chef. I am not a nutritionist. I am not a scientist. And, I am not intimidated by that. I proudly admit that I am a self-taught cook who can now create delectable meals from nutritious whole foods. You don't have to be classically trained in order to feed yourself well. Life is complicated. Food is simple.

I didn't know that my career would take off in this direction. My passion for food and curiosity in finding life balance led me to where I am today. I became a wellness coach and wrote this book because I want to empower others to organize their thoughts and reach their wellness goals.

For all my friends and coworkers out there who curiously leaned over my cubical wall and incessantly inquired, "What are you eating?" "That smells so good." "Did you make that?" "Can I taste it?" "Ooh, Malia, I need that recipe!"–this is for you.

Relax and smile. I am going to the store with you.

Malia Dell

INTRODUCTION

Who is this for?

Food That Works is for health-conscious or wannabe-health-conscious people on the go. This is a Monday-through-Friday cookbook. It is for working professionals who commute, have limited time, and just need a plan to survive the hectic workweek. It is also for people who are intimidated by cooking and who crave basic know-how and guidance. Most of us work long hours and need fast, healthful, portable breakfasts and lunches. And when we get home at night, we deserve easy delicious dinners. **Having a busy schedule does not mean we must compromise our health and settle for subpar meals in a restaurant or from a cardboard box or drive-thru window.** I created this system so you don't have to think. You can go to the store with a shopping list and come home with a plan for the *whole week*. My Shopping Lists were designed for a household of two, with leftovers, but can easily be modified by purchasing more or fewer ingredients. Whether you are a recent graduate just starting out on your own or part of a busy household just looking for some new quick and simple meal ideas, we all could use a little *Food That Works*.

How is this cookbook different?

This cookbook was designed around the real life factors that prevent us from cooking for ourselves. Food shopping, recipes, planning what the hell to eat, and cleaning up are things we just don't have time for during the weekly grind. *Food That Works* considers all of the above and offers a food system. Outlined in five weekly plans, the food system helps you navigate through these obstacles. Other cookbooks are designed to serve one purpose, which they do beautifully, and that is to provide you with an outstanding meal. Unfortunately, the recipes in those books are disjointed. They call for ingredients that don't cross over from one recipe to the next, leaving you with a bunch of random leftover

WHAT DOES THIS COOKBOOK DO?

- Guides you toward eating more meals prepared at home and fewer meals out.

- Offers you five great weekly menus to choose from, all paired with shopping lists and recipes.

- Strategically uses up all the ingredients purchased—NO WASTE.

- Encourages you to read ingredients labels, select the best quality ingredients, and move away from processed and packaged foods.

- Teaches you how to prep, keep food in rotation, and run your kitchen efficiently—like a restaurant.

- Provides healthful recipes for the meals you already know and love (burgers, tacos, chili, BBQ chicken), all designed to have minimal clean up.

ingredients and a one-off meal that took hours to prepare and clean up after. This is clearly not helpful for busy people. *Food That Works* is a survival cookbook that stands up to the demands of a workweek; not just a book that you can utilize during luxurious hours of free time on weekends.

Not all of my techniques are glamorous, but they work. Sometimes, in the comfort of your own home, you just need to be able to slam some good food down your gullet and move on. In reality, good cooking is pretty damn basic. But you have to get in there, get your hands wet, and DO IT. Be courageous. Once you create a few successful meals, your confidence will grow. With repetition, you get better. You will keep going, and keep trying out new

recipes until one day…Dang! You don't even need a recipe; you just know how to make <enter favorite meal here>. Let this book set you free. I tear down the misconceptions that cooking is difficult, that recipes are finite, and that daily meals need to be ostentatious productions.

What *are* you eating?

Sadly, the craft of home cooking is fading rapidly. Today, packaged food, prepared by "someone else" is accepted as the norm and is now the basis of the food culture in America. Because of this, we have the illusion that it must be too difficult and time-consuming to prepare our own food, so we better just buy it packaged in a box or in a jar. We do not ask, "W*hat is in this? How was this created? Why must it have all these strange additives in it? How much time has passed from when this was produced to the moment it touches my lips? Weeks? Months?"* I have no clue.

> "All of us work in repetitive jobs, the same faces, phone calls, and meetings … we face the incessant repetition of the modern age. We need outlets for creativity; we need to stretch our fingers and make something. And cooking is, in its essence, creating …. So set yourself free in the kitchen—once you've got some cooking know-how."
>
> **Bruce Weinstein and Mark Scarbrough, cookbook authors and food writers**

"it's hard to imagine ever reforming the American way of eating or, for that matter, the American food system unless millions of Americans—women and men—are willing to make cooking a part of daily life. The path to a diet of fresher, unprocessed food, not to mention to a revitalized local-food economy, passes straight through the home kitchen."

Michael Pollan, author, journalist, professor and activist

Each time we buy the packaged versions of the foods we love, we sign up for subpar added ingredients: fat, sugar, salt, and preservatives. We do this with *so* many food products that we have increased our consumption of these additives to excessive amounts. Does it seem right for our bodies to be bogged down processing these extra substances day in and day out, robbing us of our precious energy?

Not until you touch your food can you truly understand what is *in* your food. Then the connection will be made as to why *only* the best quality ingredients will suffice to make up *your* food. Smile, this is going to be *much* more enjoyable than you *ever* expected.

Easy Does It

Learning to eat healthfully is a journey. It has taken our entire lives up to this very moment to form our food habits, so we cannot realistically expect to change everything in our diets overnight. Eating healthfully comes with cumulative changes made over time. This is why restrictive diets fail: they are too extreme—too much at once. Let this book ease you into informed shopping and healthful eating gradually, one small ingredient substitution at a time. If you despise whole wheat pasta, then stick to regular pasta. What matters is that you are in your kitchen, cooking fresh food for yourself. That should be your primary objective. You will adopt the foods you prefer and the habits that speak to you, and you will shed the rest.

Once you've learned the *Food That Works* techniques, you can use them with any recipe that appeals to you, whether it's from a friend, a blog, or another cookbook.

"Growth is not steady, forward, upward progression. It is instead a switchback trail; three steps forward, two back, one around the bushes, a few simply standing, before another forward leap."

Dorothy Corkille Briggs, teacher, school psychologist and dean of schools

Hey, are you gonna eat that?

Does food waste make you furious? It should. The recipe for avoiding household food waste is simple: you need a dash of creativity, a drop of food knowledge, and an ounce of respect.

If we want to live in a sustainable world, we need to change the way we consume our natural resources, including those that go into our food.

If you are guilty of weekly food waste, there is a reason this book found its way into your hands. Household food waste *is* avoidable, and it is time for all virtuous home cooks to recognize and repurpose their surplus.

Here are the best ways to combat food waste at the household level:
- Stick to a shopping list
- Store food properly
- Run an organized, uncluttered fridge
- Keep food in rotation by using items that will perish first
- Increase your knowledge of ways to use ingredients across multiple meals
- Freeze surplus leftovers (and actually eat them!)

You start to play a little game in your head: "Ok, I need to use that broccoli and I have a can of tomatoes; let's see if I can rustle up some pasta, and *boom*, dinner." "These bananas are turning brown, I will peel and freeze them for future smoothies before they go bad." "There is no way I will eat all this mac & cheese, I'll bring some in for my coworkers tomorrow." **It is extremely gratifying when you figure out ways to utilize every item with the utmost efficiency.**

Damn, you're good.

I hope to bring awareness to the issue of food waste and cause each of us to evaluate our own habits. We can all do better. Be thrifty and resourceful in your kitchen.

Whatever reason motivates you, whether it's economic, environmental, or ethical, **I beg you, respect food. If you buy it, use it.**

Studies show that swearing in a nonabusive manner in the workplace improves morale, helps coworkers feel like a cohesive group, and relieves stress. So let those bombs fly! Of course, swearing like a pro requires timing and tact. You'll get there. I practice in the car . . . a lot!

"We, the people, do have the power to stop [the] tragic waste of resources if we regard it as socially unacceptable to waste food."

Tristram Stuart, author and campaigner against food waste

Run it like a restaurant!

Chefs know exactly what is in their fridge, what they can make from those ingredients, and what they need to use up first before it goes bad. Restaurants refer to this as "rotation," or first in first out (FIFO), and home cooks need to do the same. Eventually, this thinking will become second nature for you, and you will begin to **run your kitchen like an efficient restaurant.** 86 waste!

In my house, when I swing open the fridge door, it is never a question of *what* should I eat? The question is always obvious: what should I eat *first*? As you cook your way through this book, you will spend more time handling fresh produce, you will connect to your food, and you will realize a sense of urgency above all else, an innate duty, to put that food to good use.

Leftovers Love Affair

If you don't *love* leftovers, you will. Leftovers don't have to be a dull repeat; this book teaches you to get back in there and serve them up as new creations. Leftovers are gold nuggets of deliciousness that save

Food
1 = buy it with thought
2 = cook it with care
3 = serve just enough
4 = save what will keep
5 = eat what would spoil
6 = home-grown is best

don't waste it

COMMITTEE OF PUBLIC SAFETY, DEPARTMENT OF FOOD SUPPLY, SOUTH PENN SQUARE, PHILADELPHIA

Bring Your Own Food (BYOF) wherever you go. This allows you to control the ingredients, avoid restaurant-size portions (which often go to waste), and save you stacks of cash. Start to BYOF to work, and your coworkers will get all drooly with envy, wondering how you have time to pack such bomb lunches every day. My advice? Hide your stash well to avoid lunchroom theft, and get your coworkers their own copies of *Food That Works*!

 you money and time, so throughout this book they are labeled with a little pot of gold. By cooking extra food with the intention of having leftovers, you are getting the cutting board out only once, cleaning up only once, and benefiting with several meals ready to go. Besides, what is better than enjoying a delicious meal? Enjoying it twice. **CHA-CHING!**

IMPORTANT: Every ingredient in this book is optional.

I repeat, optional. That's right, if you don't like it, don't buy it. Please replace it with something else, something similar, something you like! I deliberately included a variety of foods in this book so you would try new things. But my feelings won't be hurt if you stray. Perhaps the most liberating part of

cooking is the ability to **modify anything you want to be exactly the way you like it.**

My recipes are guidelines; you are the cook! I give you permission to taste and lead with your tongue. It is your preference, your groceries, your dinner. If you don't like peppers, substitute another vegetable, say, zucchini. Don't like salmon? Use another type of fish. Substitute your freaking heart out. Let me know how it turns out!

> *"I learned to cook in order to get away from recipes."*
>
> **Tom Colicchio, award-winning chef, restaurateur, and Top Chef host**

HOW TO USE THIS BOOK

1. Pick a Week

There are five Weeks to choose from, each having a different color and different flavors. Each Week includes a Shopping List, Prep Day instructions, a menu listing the many meals you can assemble from those ingredients, and delicious quick recipes. The Weeks were designed to be flexible, because, true to life, every week is different. Simply select the Week that complements your schedule; some Weeks are shorter than others. To ease into your new habit of cooking from home, you can follow the Weeks in order, or you can skip around to whichever Week's menu sounds most delicious to you.

2. Shop from the List

Pantry Must-Haves: Each Shopping List starts with your Pantry Must-Haves. These are the essentials, like flour, oil, and spices, that are needed for *all* the recipes that Week. **You probably already have many of these items.** Each list provides the quantities needed for the week to avoid duplicate purchases. Yes, yes, I did all that sweet math for you. Now, take inventory of your pantry and fridge *before* you go shopping!

Shopping List: Take the Shopping List to the store with you. It may seem daunting at first to shop from someone else's list, but trust my system; I have done the thinking for you. FYI–Shopping Lists can be printed off of the *Food That Works* website (foodthatworks.info).

Food Selection: The Ingredients Guide on page 143 and the information about buying organic on page 44 will help you choose the best quality products. The more you know, the better decisions you can make at the store. I *urge you* to start reading and questioning the ingredients in your food, in effect, changing the way you shop.

Always select the product that has the fewest listed ingredients. Fewer ingredients = less processed.

3. Get Through Prep Day

I can't stress enough the importance of busting through as much of the Prep Day instructions as you can. The biggest mistake people are making is returning home from the store, putting everything away, and opening a bag of chips, never taking the time to prep and actually cook the food they bought. If you want fast meals throughout the week, prepping ingredients is essential. Restaurants do it, and you should too. This preparation is why *Food That Works* works!

If you commit to one to two hours of prep at the beginning of your week, you will cruise through the recipes in this book as they were intended. Some weeks you might prep better than others, but the goal is to make prep work an effortless part of your kitchen routine. Then you can turn to your *fast fridge* instead of fast food when you are hungry!

4. Don't Think—Cook!

Your stomach growls, you open the fridge, you assemble the meal. Depending on what you are in the mood for, you flip to a recipe and *cook!* You've already done a lot of prep work, so full-on recipes like chili and burgers will take only half the time to make. A handful of this, a handful of that, and voilà, your kickass dinner is ready! These recipes have minimal steps, and minimal clean up–because who has time to clean? You're welcome.

5. Use Every Crumb

At the end of the week, your fridge should look pretty bare and clean! That's good! You have successfully utilized everything you purchased. Now pick a new Week and REPEAT!

IMPORTANT TIPS TO SHOP AND EAT BY

IT IS TIME to start giving a fork about what is in your food. I do not preach about tracking carbs, reducing sodium, or counting calories, points, grams, what-have-you. That is up to you if you enjoy tracking those things. I was never one for numbers, or rules for that matter. (Wink) So I kept this list short. Embody these tips and you are on the path to healthful eating. The goal is to move away from mindlessly buying packaged and processed convenience foods and to ease into the world of home cooking with fresh whole ingredients instead.

"Use the best products: then you can serve them simply."

Mimi Thorisson, cookbook author and food blogger

AS OFTEN AS POSSIBLE:

Read Ingredients Labels—Brand, package—none of that matters. All you care about is the ingredients label. A long list indicates that it is highly processed, put it back. Shoot for 10 ingredients or fewer. Compare different brands and select the one with the fewest listed ingredients. For example, a can of beans should read "Ingredients: beans, water, salt." Clean and simple.

Buy Single-Ingredient Foods— Potatoes, peppers, tomatoes, apples, beans—foods you can picture growing in nature—these are whole foods. You will be pleasantly surprised when you look down at your cart and see that it is filled with more single-ingredient, recognizable, foods and less ink and advertising.

Refuse to Buy—Don't buy anything that lists "high fructose" or "hydrogenated" in the ingredients list. I don't subscribe to many rules in life, but this one I *never* break. Simply decide to eliminate these from your diet and you are already winning.

Stick to the List—These lists will prevent impulse purchases and allow for quick navigation through the store. Stick to your mission, in and out.

Buy Organic—Eating organic foods reduces pesticide intake and gives you superior flavor. *Especially* with produce, make the splurge for organic. You are worth it. For more on buying organic, see page 44.

If you have a question about an ingredient, look it up in the Ingredients Guide on page 143.

WARNING

After cooking through this book, you may become an ingredient snob.

PREPARATION GUIDE

For some of you, the Prep Day may seem intimidating at first. But it will get easier with practice, and I promise you will learn a ton along the way. Save yourself the hassle–remember these four tips:

- Whenever chopping, use a large chef's knife.
- A sharp knife will save you hours in the kitchen.
- Ingredients cut into uniform sizes will cook evenly.
- Don't take yourself too seriously. Seriously.

Roughly Chop large pieces, about 1 inch

Finely Chop small pieces, about ¼ inch

Chop medium pieces, about ¾ inch (The most common dice size in this book)

Mince smallest of all (Achieved by rocking a chef's knife back and forth over the pieces)

Cube to cut food into uniform squares.

Drain to pour off the water or liquid from food, usually through a colander or strainer. For example, draining the water after pasta is cooked. Remember to tip the pot away from you to avoid getting steam in your face!

Grate to reduce a large piece of food into small bits by rubbing it on the small holes of a grater. In this book, the small holes on the grater are used to grate ginger or citrus zest. Also see zest.

Peel Garlic to remove the papery protective skin. Dislodge the individual cloves from the garlic head. Place a clove under the flat side of a chef's knife, and

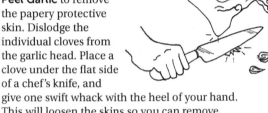

give one swift whack with the heel of your hand. This will loosen the skins so you can remove them with your fingers.

Pulse to chop food into smaller bits in a blender or food processor. Pulsing is done by pushing and releasing the power or pulse button in short bursts, about 2 seconds. Pulse several times until the food is chopped to the desired size.

Puree to blend food until it is completely smooth and free of lumps. In this book, pureeing is done with a hand immersion blender to make smoothies, hummus, and brownie batter. Soups and sauces can be partially pureed, leaving some chunks if you don't want it completely smooth. Pureeing can also be done in a food processor or blender.

Shred to reduce a large piece of food into thin strips by rubbing it on the large holes of a grater. In this book, the large holes on the grater are used to shred cheese, carrots, potatoes, and onions. Cooked meat can be shredded by pulling it apart with a fork.

Zest to finely grate the top layer of the skin of a citrus fruit on the small holes of a grater. The zest contains the fruit's oils and bright flavor but not the acidity. Grate the colorful skin of the fruit down to the white part then move on to another section. The white pith is bitter and should not be included in your zest.

Chop Like A Boss

I never enjoyed cooking until I learned how to chop efficiently. I especially hated cutting onions, so I taught myself the fastest way to chop an onion by watching a video on Youtube. It changed my life. So do yourself a favor–master this technique and apply it to *any* vegetable you chop. It becomes a fun little challenge to figure out how to chop an item with the fewest cuts, and it will save you countless hours and tears. Go now with the quickness!

1. Cut the top off the onion, but leave the hairy root side. The root will keep the onion intact while you chop.

2. Cut the onion in half lengthwise, right through the root to top. Now you have two halves.

3. Peel off the skin and first layer of the onion on each half.

4. Lay the cut-side down on the cutting board. Carefully make three incisions parallel to the cutting board, cutting three-fourths of the way without cutting through the root end.

5. Next, following the lines on the onion, make incisions without cutting through the root. The space between the cuts will determine the size of the final pieces. Make incisions far apart, about ½ inch, for a chop, and closer together, about ⅛ inch, for a fine chop.

6. Now slice the onion in the opposite direction, across the cuts you've already made. The onion will fall into a beautiful dice (with minimal cuts) due to its natural layers. Again, the space between the cuts will determine the size of the final pieces. Repeat with the other half.

COOKING TERMS

The following cooking terms are defined as they are referred to in this book.

Bake/Roast: Baking or roasting takes place in the oven. The oven's enclosed high heat browns the surface of the food, which concentrates flavors, caramelizes carbs, and brings out the sugary side in vegetables. These two terms can be used interchangeably, although roasting typically boasts higher temperatures, deeper browning, and faster cooking. For one example, see Green Prep Day instructions for baked chicken breasts on page 98.

Boil: Boiling takes place on the stovetop. Water boils at 212°F, at which time it will be bubbling and turning to vapor. This thrashing and bubbling is referred to as a "rolling boil." Typically, after water comes to a boil, the heat is turned down to low or medium so that there are fewer bubbles appearing on the surface, keeping it at a *simmer*. A rolling boil is too harsh an environment to add food; the food will quickly become tough, flavorless, or fall apart. For one example, see pasta directions in Pasta Salad on page 128.

Broil: Broiling takes place in the oven. Broiling is cooking food at an extremely high temperature, around 500°F, very close to the heat source, which gives the food a crispy exterior with a charred look and flavor. The effects of broiling are similar to what you would get on a grill. It is important to get the food you are broiling as close as possible to the red-hot heat source, within two inches, by placing it on the highest oven rack. This cooks the food quickly so it is important never to walk away from food that is broiling and to constantly keep checking on it and flipping it when necessary. Always leave the oven door ajar while broiling; this prevents your oven from overheating and serves as a reminder to check your food. For one example, see Charbroiled Vegetables on page 54.

Pan-Fry: Pan-frying takes place on the stovetop. Pan-frying is similar to sautéing because you are starting with hot oil in a hot pan. But pan-frying uses slightly more oil, slightly lower temperature, less tossing, and longer cooking time. That is why pan-frying is a good method for cooking meat as it allows enough time for the meat to cook through and also get a little brown on the outside. For one example, see Turkey Burgers on page 89.

Roux (roo): Making a roux takes place on the stovetop. A roux is a thickener made by whisking a fat, like butter, and flour continually over medium to high heat until a thick, bubbly magic happens. Don't walk away; you must constantly attend to a roux so it doesn't burn! Roux is used to thicken sauces, gravies, and soups. For one example, see White Bean Chicken Chili on page 42.

Sauté: Sautéing takes place on the stovetop. Sautéing is cooking food very quickly in a small amount of oil in a very hot pan. This high heat browns the food's surface and brings out its complex flavors and aromas. When sautéing, it's important to heat the oil before adding the food to the pan. Another key is to keep tossing and flipping the food in the pan, quickly and often, to ensure that it cooks evenly and does not stick. Avoid crowding the food in the pan; too much food in the pan causes it to steam rather than sauté. Keep the pieces in one layer, and don't let them touch each other. For one example, see Quick Omelet aka Quomelet on page 102.

Steam: Steaming takes place on the stovetop. Steaming is a quick cooking method using moist heat (hot steam) to gently cook the food. A pot is filled with 1 inch of water, and brought to a boil. A steamer basket is inserted to keep the vegetables suspended above the water. Vegetables are then added, covered with a tight lid, and steamed for 2 to 7 minutes, just until the vegetables are bright and crisp. Overcooking vegetables leaves them limp, flavorless, and with a strange odor, which is why steamed vegetables have such a bad rep. Always aim to undercook your vegetables; cook them "al dente." For one example, see Steamed Summer Squash on page 67.

Steam in parchment paper aka *en papillote*: This technique involves enclosing food in a packet of parchment paper, then heating it in the oven for roughly 10 to 15 minutes, so that the food cooks in its own steam. The key is a well-folded seal on the paper packet so the steam does not escape. I included this method because it is quick, no fuss, and yields moist, perfect results every time with very little clean up. This method is used most often for cooking fish and vegetables.

KITCHEN UTENSILS

IN THIS SECTION, I will not tell you to run out and buy a ton of stuff before you can start eating healthfully. I haven't been in your kitchen, but I'd like to think we can get creative and work with what you've already got. Listed below are useful items for the recipes in this book and other everyday cooking. Upgrading your kitchen tools is something that will happen gradually, one new item at a time, as you cook more and realize what items are *truly* worth the investment for you. It's not the number of fancy gadgets you have that makes you a good cook. Successful cooks have their basic utensils in reachable spots while they are cooking. It's that simple. So before you run out and spend a ton of money, think minimalist kitchen. I pride myself on my minimal collection. I can strategically pack my whole kitchen into two boxes. Thus, I had no problem stripping this list down to its skivvies for you.

Baking pans (glass, ceramic, or tin)–
Large baking dish: 11- by 7-inch or 13- by 9-inch
Large baking sheet
Loaf pan: 8- by 4-inch or 9- by 5-inch
Medium baking dish: 8-inch square
Muffin tin
Pie dish: 9- or 10-inch round

Chef's knife–the only knife you need. A sharp chef's knife will help you breeze through your Prep Day chopping. Well worth the investment. Get one with a handle that feels good in your hand and does a comfortable rocking motion on the cutting board.

Cooking pots–
Large pot with lid: 4½-quart
Medium pot with lid: 3-quart
Small pot with lid: 2-quart
Lids don't need to fit exactly, I never bother reaching for the "right" lid. Just use what you've got; I've even used a plate.

Cutting boards–at least one large, plastic or wood

Dish towels–tucked into your pants, belt loop, or apron strings whenever you're in the kitchen. It will be there whenever you need to wipe the counter or your hands fifty million times. Please stop destroying the earth and creating waste with paper towels. Cringe.

> ## Tip
>
> With the amount of cooking you will be doing, I suggest you evolve past a salt shaker. Instead, keep a small dish of salt conveniently near the stove so you can quickly add pinches as needed.

Disposables–
Parchment paper–located in the tin foil aisle. It is parchment paper, not wax paper. You cannot cook with wax paper!
Plastic storage bags
Plastic wrap
Tin foil

Frying pans (nonstick)–
Large frying pan: 10- to 12-inch
Small frying pan: 6- to 8-inch

Grater–four-sided hand grater

Hand immersion blender (my all-time favorite tool)–pretty much the ONLY tool *I will* tell you to go out to buy if you want to eat healthfully on the fly. A normal blender or food processor will suffice; it just has more parts to clean. The hand immersion blender can go directly in the pot to puree your favorite soup or in your cup to whip up a morning smoothie, and you have only one part, to clean. I recommend a good stainless steel Cuisinart model priced at $60.00 to $70.00 dollars. If you plan to chop ice, get the more expensive model. ¿Qué? Did someone say margaritas?

Masking tape and permanent marker–use masking tape to label and date leftovers and frozen meals. (That is what restaurants do!) Then everyone in your house will know what is available, and they will be more inclined to eat it. While you're at it, label the cabinets, fridge shelves, and pantry. Signage makes the world go round. Create a system that works for your household, communicate it, enforce it, and reinforce it with labels!

Measuring cups and Measuring spoons

Reusable to-go containers and assorted glass jars–for free storage containers, keep your wide-mouth glass peanut butter jars and plastic

>
> **Tip**
> Do not heat food in the microwave in plastic containers. When hot food comes in contact with plastic, it causes harmful chemicals from the plastic to leach into the food. Food should always be transferred to a glass or ceramic plate before microwaving it.

>
> **Tip**
> Rearrange your cabinets, drawers and countertops so the items you use the most take up the best real estate in your kitchen. Make it more functional to work in your space. Box up all the other appliances, duplicate bowls, and dusty china set, and move them to the basement, or better yet, the thrift store.

containers from yogurt and cottage cheese. The 32-ounce yogurt containers are the perfect vessels to blend up Smoothies in with the hand immersion blender. When you really start to BYOF, you might consider slowly adding a few glass storage containers to your collection, making the shift away from plastic. Glass containers last forever, are BPA free, easy to clean, and don't stain or retain odors. I recommend Glasslock storage containers with the Snaplock lids. These glass containers are leakproof due to their sturdy plastic lids that securely latch on all four sides. I let these babies tumble around in my luggage and purse–no leaks! They are shatterproof, microwaveable, and some are even ovenproof. Every month or two, I would treat myself to a new Glasslock container, and by the end of the year, I had what I needed.

Rice Cooker (3-cup or less)–a great timesaver that will ensure perfect rice every time. Cooking rice can be

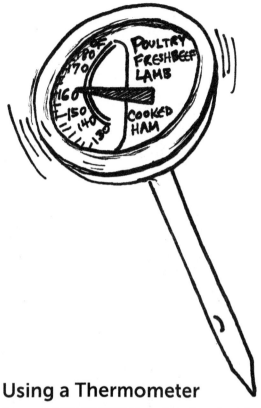

finicky, no matter how long you've been cooking. It doesn't always turn out right: too mushy, excess water, undercooked, burnt! Throw on your rice cooker; go throw on your comfy clothes–dinner is almost ready.

Music, wine, apron!

Enjoy what you are doing. If you dread peeling potatoes, pull up a chair and blast your favorite tunes or make your <boyfriend, girlfriend, husband, wife, partner, friend> do it. A glass of wine always makes for a nice accompaniment while you're in the kitchen. I have a beloved apron, and aside from its obvious purpose, it looks cute. This is your quiet time in the kitchen, experimenting, creating, and learning. Food always tastes better when the cook enjoyed making it. When I am rushing, cursing, spilling, and burning things, even my food tastes angry.

Timer–If you are like me and like to multitask, get into the habit of setting a timer so you don't burn everything to sh*%.

Using a Thermometer

It is especially important to cook beef, pork, and poultry to a safe temperature to kill off illness-causing bacteria. Many home cooks, like me, don't use thermometers for everyday cooking and feel comfortable cutting into the center of meat to carefully inspect it for doneness. When cooking big cuts of meat like a pork roast or a whole turkey, I absolutely use a thermometer, but we are not cooking anything like that in this book. Although the method of "eyeballing it" for doneness is not 100 percent accurate, I believe it is extremely important to know what to look for and how to gauge doneness yourself in case you do not have access to a thermometer. What would you do? Starve? No, no. I tell you what to look for and how to carefully check meat for doneness.

A surefire way to know if meat is done is to take its internal temperature with a thermometer. It takes out the guesswork and puts you at ease. I suggest you buy a simple bimetallic stemmed thermometer, and teach yourself how to use it properly. FYI–Poultry is fully cooked when a thermometer inserted in the thickest part registers 165°F.

Malia, Chicago,
summer 1992

Take a leap...

Ciao Bella!

Red Week

AKA THE SHORT WEEK

MENU

∿∿∿

Theme: Italian American
Prep Day Length: 1½ hours
Total Meals for the Week: 50%

∿∿∿

PREP DAY RECIPE
Hard-Boiled Eggs, *p. 35*

BREAKFAST
Greek Yogurt Bowl with Fruit, Nuts, and Honey, *p. 36*
Home Fries served with Fried Eggs, *p. 36*
Quick Omelet aka Quomelet, *p. 102*
Smoothies, *p. 124*

LUNCH
Buffalo Chicken Salad, *p. 37*
Waldorf Salad with Raspberry Vinaigrette, *p. 38*
Leftovers from Dinner:
Blue Fettuccini Alfredo
Eggplant Polenta Bake
White Bean Chicken Chili

DINNER
Blue Fettuccini Alfredo, *p. 39*
Eggplant Polenta Bake, *p. 40*
Pasta Primavera, *p. 41*
White Bean Chicken Chili, *p. 42*

EXTRAS
Loaded Baked Potato (optional), *p. 43*

PANTRY MUST-HAVES

Items and quantities needed for this entire Week. Do you have them?

FLOUR, PREFERABLY WHOLE WHEAT
½ cup

HONEY
2 tablespoons

UNSALTED BUTTER
1½ sticks
(12 tablespoons)

EXTRA VIRGIN OLIVE OIL, COLD-PRESSED
¾ cup

BRAGGS LIQUID AMINOS
2 tablespoons

WORCESTERSHIRE SAUCE
1 tablespoon

APPLE CIDER VINEGAR, UNFILTERED
2 tablespoons

CAYENNE PEPPER

CHILI POWDER

CINNAMON, GROUND

CUMIN, GROUND

CURRY POWDER

OREGANO LEAVES, DRIED

PEPPER

RED PEPPER FLAKES

SALT

RED SHOPPING LIST

Read your labels! Make sure every item you put in your cart is
Food That Works approved. See page 18.

Fruit

*Granny Smith apple: 1

*Red grapes: 1 small bag

Vegetables

*Baby spinach: 1 (5-ounce) tub

*Baby spinach: 1 (5-ounce) bag

*Large-leaf spinach: 1 (8-ounce) bag

*Grape tomatoes: 1 pint

Garlic: 2 heads

*Celery: 1 (10-ounce) bag

Yellow onions: 2

Red onion: 1 small

*Green bell pepper: 1

*Red bell pepper: 1

Summer squash aka yellow squash: 1

Eggplant: 1 medium

*Russet potatoes: 2 of equal size

Fresh Herbs

Scallions: 1 bunch

Specialty Cheese Section

Parmesan cheese: 1 (8- to 10-ounce) wedge

Blue cheese, Gorgonzola, or Roquefort: 1 (6- to 8-ounce) wedge

Fresh mozzarella: 1 (8-ounce) ball

Poultry

*Chicken breasts, boneless skinless: 1½ pounds

Pasta, Grains, Nuts

Pasta, preferably whole wheat, fettuccini, linguini, or penne: 1 (12-ounce) box

Brown rice, preferably Basmati: 1 (2-pound) bag

Cornmeal, stone ground, medium- or coarse-ground: 1 (2-pound) bag

Walnuts, chopped: 1 (8-ounce) bag

Cans, Jars, Bottles & More

Cannellini beans or any white bean: 2 (15-ounce) cans

Chipotle peppers in adobo sauce: 1 (4-ounce) can

Spaghetti sauce: 1 (24-ounce) jar

Buffalo sauce: 1 bottle (any size), like Frank's RedHot Buffalo Wing Sauce

Raspberry preserves or jam: 1 jar (any size)

Vanilla protein powder: 1 container (any size) (optional for Smoothies)

Refrigerated

Cottage cheese, any style: 1 (16-ounce) container, like Hood Cottage Cheese and Chive

Greek yogurt, plain, full-fat: 1 (32-ounce) container

*Eggs: 1 dozen

Almond milk, unsweetened, or milk of your choice: 1 (half gallon) carton

Frozen

*Berries: 1 (15-ounce) bag

Asterisk (*) suggests to buy organic

RED PREP DAY

NOW YOU HAVE ALL OF YOUR GROCERIES. With a little forethought, you will have quick and healthful meals waiting in your fridge for the busy week ahead. This prep list is strategically designed to get you through this process efficiently; do as much as you can. Ready to multitask? Put on some music. Here we go! We are going to bust through this.

Decide what you want to make for dinner tonight. Keep in mind that after the prep work is completed, you may want something quick and easy.

Suggestion: Blue Fettuccini Alfredo (page 39).

You will need: measuring cups, measuring spoons, large cutting board with a medium bowl next to it for scraps, chef's knife, grater, and containers and plastic bags to store chopped veggies.

Prep List:
1. Bake potatoes
2. Bake chicken breasts
3. Hard boil eggs
4. Chop vegetables
5. Shred Parmesan cheese
   Peel garlic (optional)

Preheat oven to Bake 350°F to bake the potatoes and chicken breasts.
Position a rack in the middle of the oven.

1. Bake potatoes:

2 potatoes—scrub well, dry with a towel. Gently stab each potato several times with a fork to prevent exploding—you know how I feel about cleaning. Use your hands to rub the potatoes with a little olive oil. This makes the skins easy to peel. Lay a sheet of tin foil directly on the oven rack to one side and place the greased potatoes on it. These will bake 50 to 60 minutes depending on size. There will be a slight give to the potato when it is done.

2. Bake chicken breasts:

Two breasts will be for White Bean Chicken Chili, and the third will be for Buffalo Chicken Salad.

Line a large baking sheet with tin foil.

Using one hand, place three chicken breasts on the baking sheet. Using your clean hand, generously salt and pepper both sides of the breasts. Lightly drizzle olive oil on the breasts, and rub it around with your hands to coat them. This creates a barrier to hold in the moisture, preventing chicken from drying out during the baking process. Thoroughly wash your hands and any other items that came in contact with raw chicken.

 Place the chicken in the oven next to the two potatoes, bake 25 to 30 minutes, depending on size; set timer.

Tip

Whenever necessary, pound chicken breasts to equal thickness so they cook evenly. Place them between two pieces of plastic wrap, and beat them with a heavy object, like the back of a heavy spoon, a rolling pin, or a meat mallet, until they are roughly the same thickness.

3. Hard boil eggs:

Hard-Boiled Eggs (page 35).

4. Chop vegetables:

For definitions of chop, mince, zest, etc., see page 20.

Summer squash:
1 summer squash–remove and discard the stem and end into the scrap bowl. Slice the summer squash into ½-inch thick rounds. Store in a plastic bag in the refrigerator. Use within 5 to 6 days.

Bell peppers:
1 green bell pepper and 1 red bell pepper–remove stems, core, and seeds; discard them in the scrap bowl. Chop the peppers and store them together in a container in the refrigerator. Use within 5 to 6 days.

How is that chicken doing?

Once the timer goes off, remove the chicken from the oven and cut into the middle of one breast to check for doneness. The center should be juicy, white, and cooked through, not pink. If it is still pink, cook another 5 to 10 minutes. Allow the chicken to cool completely before storing. Store in a container in the refrigerator. Use within 4 days.

 Set timer for another 30 minutes, so you don't forget about the potatoes.

Chop vegetables continued...

Onions:
Forgive me now for your crying eyes. I know this is a lot of onions to chop. But during the week when you can quickly add chopped onions into recipes, you will love me again. PAIN & GLORY! For the fastest way to chop an onion, see page 21.

2 yellow onions–chop and store in a container in the refrigerator. Use within 7 days.

1 red onion–finely chop and store in a container in the refrigerator. Use within 7 days.

5. Shred Parmesan cheese:

Shred on the large holes of a grater (about 1½ cups) for quick access during the week. Store in the refrigerator in a plastic bag with the air removed. Use within 7 days.

Once the timer goes off, the potatoes should be easily pierced in the middle with a fork. If they are still hard in the middle, then cook an additional 15 minutes. Allow the potatoes to cool completely before storing. Store wrapped in tin foil or in a plastic bag in the refrigerator. Use within 3 to 4 days.

Done! Your fridge should look awesome and organized.

Feeling ambitious?

Peel about 20 cloves of garlic now to save you time during the week. Store in a container in the refrigerator. Use within 7 days. For instructions on peeling garlic, see page 20.

Reuse your scraps!

Reduce the amount of trash and landfill waste you produce by repurposing the vegetable matter in your scrap bowl.

Feed Yourself: Toss your veggie scraps into a bag in the freezer and keep adding to it each week. Once it is full, use it to make a delicious broth.

Feed the Soil: Find a way to compost your veggie scraps and allow them to biodegrade naturally back into the earth.

PREP DAY RECIPE

Hard-Boiled Eggs

Total Time: 20 minutes · Makes: 4-6

Hard-boiled eggs are the perfect food for busy people on the go. Always keep a designated bowl of hard-boiled eggs in your fridge so you can transform them into meals on the fly. Ate the last hard-boiled egg? Make more. This brain-boosting snack will get you through those hectic days. I enjoy them as egg salad with curry powder or chopped up and added to a green salad. Most of the time, I scarf them down with a little salt or Braggs. Perfect for breakfast when you may not have time to cook; you can still have your eggs! Not only are they versatile in the kitchen, but they travel well too! When I am traveling, I place two hard-boiled eggs in a plastic bag with a paper towel and throw it in my purse. The paper towel not only adds a little cushion to prevent severe crackage, but it also serves as a napkin later. When hunger strikes, no matter where I am–in a plane, train, or car–I crack and peel this convenient snack and place the shells right back in the plastic bag. Yes, I have received some strange looks when I pull whole meals out of my Purse Kitchen, but they are more like looks of envy, as in "Why didn't I ever think of that?" as they stare in awe at my dope prepping skills.

FYI–If hard-boiled eggs are not refrigerated, it is recommended to eat them within two hours.

4-6 eggs

Place the eggs in a small pot.

Fill with cold water until the eggs are just covered.

Bring to a boil over high heat, about 5 minutes.

Once boiling, turn off heat and let the eggs sit in the hot water for 15 minutes; set timer.

Drain the water. Cover the eggs with cold water to stop the cooking process.

Keep them in cold water until cool, about 10 minutes.

Transfer the hard-boiled eggs to a bowl and refrigerate. Use within 7 days.

USE IN:
Buffalo Chicken Salad
Snacks

Tip

Hard-boiled eggs don't need to be cooked to death. That is why some people don't like them, because the yolks are dry and chalky. Aim to undercook them a bit and the yolk will be a little oozy and soft. In Europe they serve them runny in the middle. Give it a try.

Greek Yogurt Bowl with Fruit, Nuts, and Honey

Total Time: 5 minutes · Serves: 1

This breakfast is a great way to greet your digestive tract in the morning. The probiotics in yogurt and the digestive enzymes in fruit help set up a healthy environment in the gut. Your gut is now ready for the rest of the food that you will layer in it throughout the day. Greek yogurt is an excellent source of vitamins and minerals. It is notably high in potassium, the mineral that helps build muscle tissue. Both nuts and Greek yogurt have good fats and protein, which will keep you full and energized well beyond noon. Good news: a serving of yogurt is an entire cup, so you get to enjoy a heaping bowl that is super filling.

1 cup plain full-fat Greek yogurt
1 tablespoon fruit preserves or jam (optional)
¼ cup nuts of your choice
½ cup chopped fruit (fresh, frozen, or dried)
1½ teaspoons honey or maple syrup (a nice drizzle)

Place the yogurt in a bowl.

Stir in the preserves, if using.

Top with nuts, fruit, and whatever other toppings you like.

Take a spoonful of honey, hold it high over the bowl and move your hand back and forth to get a pretty zigzag drizzle pattern.

Home Fries served with Fried Eggs

Total Time: 5 minutes · Serves: 2

Why limit this meal to breakfast? As much as this meal could coax me out of bed in the morning, it could very well tuck me into bed at night!

1-2 tablespoons unsalted butter
½ cup chopped yellow onions
1 baked potato (from Prep Day page 32), chopped into 1-inch cubes
1 teaspoon Braggs Liquid Aminos or ½ teaspoon salt
1 teaspoon Worcestershire sauce
1 teaspoon white vinegar (optional)
¼ teaspoon paprika
1 dash cayenne pepper
Salt
Pepper

Place a large nonstick frying pan over medium-high heat; add butter; spread it around.

Add the onions and potatoes; stir gently to coat.

Add the Braggs, Worcestershire sauce, vinegar, paprika, cayenne, and generous dashes of salt and pepper; stir.

Cook until golden brown, about 8 minutes. If not getting brown, add another tablespoon of butter.

Taste, add more seasonings until it tastes good to you.

Transfer to a plate, serve with two Fried Eggs, see page 80.

For easy clean up, use same hot frying pan to fry the eggs.

Try my favorite cold remedy: In a mug of hot water, add fresh ginger slices, local honey, cayenne pepper, and the juice from half a lemon. You don't have to be sick to try this elixir; it is a great anytime-pick-me-up!

LUNCH

Buffalo Chicken Salad

Total Time: 10 minutes · Serves: 2

This is where Buffalo Chicken meets Chop Salad. YUM! This salad is one of my all-time faves. I used to order it out in restaurants *a lot*. But then I realized I could make it much better at home, exactly the way I like it, and with better quality ingredients. *Psssh.*

One chicken breast split between two people may not seem like a lot of meat to you. A suggested serving of meat is about 4 ounces, so think about the size of a deck of cards. Doesn't look like much? Well your body doesn't need much at one sitting. Add this proper meat serving to the top of your already protein-dense salad of spinach, cottage cheese, and egg, and you've got yourself a filling meal.

Not a fan of Buffalo sauce? Create your own dressing. See the Extra Dressing Options.

- 1 cup cottage cheese, style of your choice
- Drizzle of Buffalo sauce or dressing of your choice
- 1 baked chicken breast, (from Prep Day page 32), sliced or cubed
- ½ cup crumbled blue cheese or cheese of your choice

- ¼ cup finely chopped red onions
- 2 Hard-Boiled Eggs (from Prep Day page 35), peeled, rinsed, dried, and chopped
- 2 ribs celery, chopped
- 2 carrots, scrubbed and shredded (optional)
- 2 scallions, light green and white parts, thinly sliced
- ½ cup grape tomatoes
- 2 large handfuls fresh baby spinach

If you are taking this salad to go, start by putting the dressing and wet ingredients at the bottom of the container so that they don't make the rest of the salad soggy.

Divide the ingredients equally between two to-go containers. Cover and refrigerate.

Before eating, shake the container vigorously to toss the salad well and combine the flavors.

Chop salads are quite beautiful; if you are serving one on a plate, arrange your toppings in neat little piles.

Extra Dressing Options
Serves 2

Creamy Blue Cheese: 4 tablespoons Greek yogurt, 2 tablespoons crumbled blue cheese, 1 dash Worcestershire sauce, ¼ teaspoon apple cider vinegar, 2 teaspoons water.

Honey BBQ: 2 tablespoons BBQ sauce, 1 teaspoon honey, ½ teaspoon apple cider vinegar, 4 teaspoons water.

Honey Mustard: 1 tablespoon honey, 2 teaspoons Dijon mustard, ½ teaspoon apple cider vinegar, 1 teaspoon water.

Raspberry Vinaigrette: See page 38.

Mix the dressing ingredients of your choice in a jar and shake vigorously, or whisk well in a bowl with a fork.

Taste, adjust seasonings to your liking. Refrigerate and use within 7 days.

Tip

Baked chicken breasts are like blank canvases to start any creative meal. You can thinly slice them for sandwiches, cube them for chicken salad, shred them into pulled chicken, or serve them whole in a hot meal.

LUNCH

Raspberry Vinaigrette:
1 tablespoon raspberry preserves or jam
1 teaspoon apple cider vinegar
2 tablespoons extra virgin olive oil

Salad:
1 Granny Smith apple, chopped
1½ cups red grapes, halved
½ cup crumbled blue cheese
½ cup chopped walnuts
2 large handfuls fresh baby spinach

If you are taking this salad to go, start by putting the dressing and wet ingredients at the bottom of the container so that they don't make the rest of the salad soggy.

Raspberry Vinaigrette:

Combine the preserves, vinegar, and olive oil in a jar; shake vigorously. Or whisk well in a bowl with a fork. Taste, and adjust seasonings to your liking.

Pour the vinaigrette into the bottom of two separate to-go containers.

Salad:

Divide the salad ingredients equally between the two containers. Cover and refrigerate.

Before eating, shake container vigorously to toss the salad well and combine the flavors.

Waldorf Salad with Raspberry Vinaigrette

Total Time: 15 minutes · Serves: 2

I love the many complementary textures and flavors of tangy cheese, crunchy walnuts, sour apples, and juicy grapes in this salad. Keeps my mouth entranced and lusting for more! Sweet raspberry vinaigrette gives this salad the perfect finish.

Store-bought dressings are expensive and loaded with calories and additives. Oftentimes, they just end up inhabiting valuable real estate in your refrigerator. By opting to make your own vinaigrette, you can modify it to your liking until you find the right balance. The combinations are endless. For more dressing options, see page 37.

Food for Thought:

I take my wellness as seriously as my career. My body is an investment and I treat it as a priority.

DINNER

Blue Fettuccini Alfredo

Total Time: 30 minutes · Serves: 4

Simple Alfredo sauce is made by simmering garlic, cheese, starchy pasta water, olive oil, and cream together. So when you read the ingredients label on jarred Alfredo sauce, you have to question why there are over *seventeen* ingredients listed. When you order this dish out, it is usually loaded with heavy cream, butter, and cheese and is extremely high in fat and calories. I have modified this recipe to be a tiny bit healthier. Learn to make your own Alfredo, and you can enjoy this rich comfy meal anytime, knowing exactly what you put in it. Keep it fresh, simple, and delicious! Being a stinky blue cheese lover, I have created this blue spin on traditional Alfredo sauce. If you are repulsed by blue cheese, I get it. It is an acquired taste. Replace the blue cheese in this recipe with good quality Parmesan. Buono!

Pasta:

2 teaspoons salt

1 (12-ounce) package whole wheat fettuccini, linguini, or penne

1 tablespoon extra virgin olive oil

1 summer squash, sliced

1 (5-ounce) bag fresh baby spinach

1½ cups grape tomatoes, halved

Alfredo Sauce:

1 tablespoon extra virgin olive oil

6-8 cloves garlic, finely chopped

1 cup unsweetened almond milk or milk of your choice

2 tablespoons flour (optional, if you want thicker sauce)

2 cups pasta water, reserved from the boiled pasta

½ cup shredded Parmesan (or 1 whole cup if you omit the blue cheese)

½ cup crumbled blue cheese

Salt

Pepper

½ cup chopped walnuts

Red pepper flakes

> **Tip**
> Next time, try substituting arugula for spinach.

Pasta:

Fill a medium pot halfway with cold water, add salt. Bring to a boil over high heat, about 5 minutes. Once boiling, reduce the heat to medium. Add the pasta, stir, and cook until tender to your liking, 6 to 8 minutes. Bite a piece to test for doneness. Remove from heat.

Set aside 2 cups of the pasta water for the Alfredo sauce. Drain the rest of the water and return the pasta to the pot.

Immediately add the olive oil; stir to coat so the noodles do not clump. Add the summer squash, spinach, and tomatoes. Stir once and cover; the heat will wilt the spinach. Set aside.

Alfredo Sauce:

Place a large nonstick frying pan over medium-high heat; add the olive oil, heat about 2 minutes. Add garlic, cook about 1 minute, stirring frequently to prevent burning. Add the almond milk, heat until bubbling, then whisk in the flour.

Slowly add the reserved pasta water, one cup at a time, whisking until thick and bubbling. Add the Parmesan and blue cheese, stir, and season with salt and pepper.

If the sauce gets too thick, add a little water, a small amount at a time, until it's the consistency you want. Pour the Alfredo Sauce on top of the pasta and veggies, and gently fold to combine. Garnish with the walnuts and red pepper flakes.

Eggplant Polenta Bake

Total Time: 45 minutes · Serves: 4

Yes! Here is some comfort food for a cold night. Polenta is a staple in traditional Italian cuisine. It's cheap, quick to make, and a nice change from your standard pasta dish. Polenta is typically made with medium- or coarse-ground cornmeal. Prepare for love at first bite.

Polenta:

1 teaspoon extra virgin olive oil, to grease baking dish
Salt
¾ cup cornmeal
3 tablespoons unsalted butter (optional)
¼ cup shredded Parmesan
Pepper

Eggplant:

1 medium eggplant
6 cloves garlic, chopped
2 tablespoons extra virgin olive oil
½ teaspoon salt

Spinach:

½ cup chopped yellow onions
1 (8-ounce) bag fresh large-leaf spinach
Salt
Pepper
Red pepper flakes

Assembly:

2 cups jarred spaghetti sauce
1 (8-ounce) ball fresh mozzarella, sliced into ½-inch rounds
1 tablespoon dried oregano
1 teaspoon red pepper flakes
Salt

Polenta is made by boiling cornmeal into a thick porridge, which then solidifies and can be baked, grilled or fried. For more on Cornmeal, see page 146.

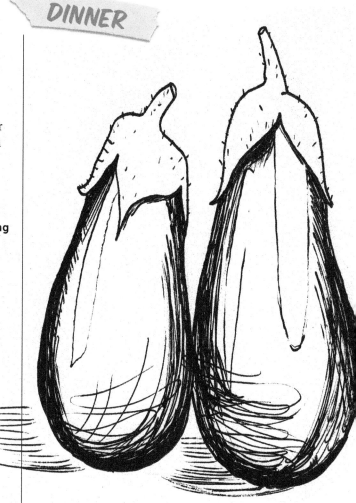

DINNER

Preheat oven to 375°F. Position one oven rack at the top, closest to the heat source, and the other rack in the middle. Grease an 8-inch square glass or ceramic baking dish with olive oil, spread with your hands or a paper towel to coat all surfaces.

Polenta:

Place 2 cups cold water and 1 teaspoon salt in a medium pot over high heat; bring to a boil.

Reduce the heat to medium-high. Slowly add the cornmeal, stirring continually with a wooden spoon in one direction to keep the mixture lump free until thick and bubbling, about 5 minutes. Remove from the heat. Add the butter and Parmesan; stir until melted. Taste and add salt and pepper to your liking.

Pour the polenta into the greased baking dish. Set aside.

Eggplant:

Line a large baking sheet with tin foil.

Wash the eggplant, remove the stem and bottom, and cut into ½-inch rounds.

In a small mixing bowl, combine the garlic, olive oil, and salt. Dip your fingers into the garlic oil and massage it onto both sides of each eggplant slice. Place the slices on the prepared baking sheet. Pour any excess garlic oil on top of the eggplant. Place the baking sheet on the middle rack of the oven. Bake 20 minutes; set timer.

Spinach:

Place a large nonstick frying pan with a lid over medium-high heat; add ¼ cup water. Once steam rises off the water, add the onions and the entire bag of spinach, tearing the leaves as you go. Cover and steam for 2 minutes. Season with salt, pepper, and red pepper flakes.

Assembly:

Place the spinach evenly on top of the polenta in the baking dish. Include the spinach juices; they are full of flavor and nutrients!

Remove the eggplant from the oven. Leave the oven on.

Add the baked eggplant on top of the spinach. It is okay if the eggplant slices overlap.

Add the spaghetti sauce, and spread it around evenly with a spoon.

Top with mozzarella. Sprinkle with oregano and red pepper flakes. Season with salt.

Cover with tin foil, and bake on the top rack for 10 minutes.

Change oven temperature to Broil–High. Remove the tin foil.

Broil until the cheese melts and turns golden brown, about 3 minutes; set timer.

Pasta Primavera

Total Time: 20 minutes · Serves: 2

You probably have some pasta kickin' around in your cabinets, and this recipe is a great way to use up that leftover jar of spaghetti sauce you might have too. Since your veggies are chopped, you can simply toss together this hot dish. Here is my ridiculously fast Pasta Primavera. *"Lay off me I'm STARVING!"* R.I.P. Chris Farley.

1 teaspoon salt
1-2 cups dried pasta (any type you have)
1½ cups jarred spaghetti sauce
1 cup chopped vegetables (like zucchini, summer squash, onions, peppers, or any other veggies you need to use up)
½ teaspoon dried oregano
1 dash red pepper flakes
Drizzle of extra virgin olive oil

Fill a medium pot halfway with cold water; add salt. Bring to a boil over high heat, about 5 minutes. Once boiling, reduce heat to medium. Add the pasta, stir, and cook until tender to your liking, 6 to 8 minutes. Bite a piece to test for doneness. Drain the pasta and return it to the pot.

Tip

Always draw water cold from the faucet for cooking and drinking, and then heat the water if desired. Hot water drawn from the faucet can more readily leach contaminants, most notably lead, from the pipes into the water.

Add the spaghetti sauce and veggies. Return the pot to medium heat. Stir and cook until the sauce is hot, about 3 minutes.

Plate and garnish with oregano, red pepper flakes, and a drizzle of olive oil.

White Bean Chicken Chili

Total Time: 1 hour · Serves: 5-6

Try this lighter version of chili, and you will be converted. Normally we think of chili as dark red and tomato based. But this chili has a white creamy base that begins with making a roux. For more instructions on making a roux, see page 22. Then we seriously season the roux with tons of rich spices and smoky chipotle peppers, which make this chili unforgettable. Careful with those chipotle peppers; they are *extremely hot!* Go ahead and bring this chili to the next party if you want a lot of press.

Rice:

2 cups brown rice (makes 4 cups cooked)

Vegetables:

1 tablespoon extra virgin olive oil
1 cup chopped onions
3 cloves garlic, chopped (1 generous tablespoon)
2 cups chopped red and green bell peppers

Roux:

4 tablespoons (½ stick) unsalted butter
¼ cup flour
1 cup unsweetened almond milk or milk of your choice
2½ cups water (or chicken broth if you have it)
1 teaspoon salt
1 teaspoon ground cumin
½ teaspoon chili powder
½ teaspoon dried oregano
1 chipotle pepper in adobo, finely chopped (2 peppers if you like it really hot)
1 tablespoon Braggs Liquid Aminos
Additional Spices: cayenne pepper for more heat, smoked paprika for smoky flavor, or a little juice from the canned chipotle peppers

Assembly:

2 (15-ounce) cans cannellini beans or any white beans, rinsed well and drained
2 baked chicken breasts (from Prep Day page 32)

Additional Toppings:

1 dollop plain full-fat Greek yogurt
Finely chopped red onions, for garnish
2 scallions, light green and white parts, thinly sliced
1 dash paprika, for color

Rice:

Place rice in a medium pot with a lid.

Fill the pot with enough cold water to cover the rice. Scrub the rice well with your hands, and pour off the water. Repeat 3 times or until water runs clear.

Add 4 cups cold water. Place over high heat; bring to a boil. Once boiling, turn heat down to medium-low, cover, and cook until tender, about 40 minutes; set timer.

Turn off the heat, and fluff with a fork. If there is excess water, pour it off. Return the rice to the warm burner and fluff with a fork until the rice dries out a bit. Cover to keep warm until ready to serve.

Vegetables:

Place a large nonstick frying pan over medium-high heat. Add the olive oil, heat about 2 minutes.

Add the yellow onions, sauté for 2 minutes. Add the garlic, and sauté 2 minutes more, stirring frequently to prevent burning.

Add the peppers, stir to combine, and sauté only 2 more minutes. You just want to lightly sauté the veggies as they will cook more in the chili. Place the veggie mixture in a bowl; set aside.

Roux:

Melt the butter in the same pan over medium heat. With a whisk, slowly add the flour to the butter. Keep breaking up the flour with the whisk, pressing up against and scraping the sides. Slowly add the almond milk. Turn the heat up to high, and whisk continually until the roux bubbles, thickens, and turns white. Continuing to whisk, slowly add the water, cup by cup, until the mixture bubbles and thickens again. Once all the water is added and the mixture is thick, reduce the heat to medium.

Stir the salt, cumin, chili powder, oregano, chipotle pepper, and Braggs into the roux. Taste and add additional spices until it tastes good to you (this is the sauce for your chili). Turn down the heat to medium-low; continue cooking.

Assembly:

Stir the rinsed beans and the vegetable mixture into the roux.

Place the baked chicken breasts on a cutting board. Use a fork to pull meat towards you with a scraping motion, shredding chicken to the desired size. Add shredded chicken to the chili; gently stir. Taste, and add a little water if it's too thick. Heat over medium-low heat for 10 minutes, or until ready to serve.

Place a serving of rice in each bowl, top with chili, then yogurt, red onions, scallions, and paprika.

Dig in!

Tip

When freezing food, always leave one inch of space at the top of the container for expansion! Label with date, type of food, and portion size. You will be more likely to eat food that is labeled. And just because it's frozen, doesn't mean you have to wait six months to eat it; bring it for lunch next week!

LEFTOVERS

Chili makes great leftovers for work. It's a "cook once; eat all week" type of meal. It freezes well and is even more delicious the second time around after the flavors have melded. Place servings of rice and chili in individual containers. Pack it down with a spoon, and tap the container on the countertop to remove any air pockets. Label and freeze. Simply reheat in a pan or microwave on a lazy night.

EXTRAS!

Loaded Baked Potato

Total Time: 5 minutes · Makes: 1

Leftover baked potatoes are like gold in my house. Bake potatoes in advance on your Prep Day, and you've created an instant baked potato bar in your fridge. When you are starving and tired, you have access to a loaded baked potato within minutes. They travel well too. So load a potato with your favorite toppings, wrap it in plastic wrap or tin foil, and reheat it at work. Getting into this habit of cooking vegetables in advance and having them in your fridge is the only way to make whole foods readily available in your busy schedule. FYI-Baked potatoes grow bacteria quickly if left out at room temperature. Keep them refrigerated, or eat them within 2 hours.

- **1 baked potato (from Prep Day page 32)**
- **1 tablespoon unsalted butter**
- **1 dollop plain full-fat Greek yogurt**
- **1 scallion, light green and white parts, thinly sliced**
- **Salt**
- **Pepper**
- **1 dash cayenne pepper or paprika (optional)**

Make a slit in the baked potato; try not to cut all the way through.

Place the butter in the slit.

Place in a microwave-safe bowl.

Heat in the microwave until the potato is hot in the middle, about 1 minute.

Top with yogurt, scallions, salt and pepper to taste, and optional spice.

Tip

If you are anti-microwave, you can reheat a baked potato in the oven. Cut the potato into fourths so it cooks faster. To prevent it from drying out, sprinkle it with a little water (just a splash or two from your fingertips), wrap it in tin foil, and bake at 400°F until warm in the middle, roughly 20 minutes.

TO BUY OR NOT TO BUY...
ORGANIC

A FEW THOUGHTS about organic…

When I told my Auntie Sandy that I could not afford to buy organic produce, she replied, "Malia, you can't afford *not* to." Her raised eyebrows and stern words have stuck with me ever since. Although I can't afford to buy *every* item organic, I do the best I can. I am worth it, and you are too. When we are talking about the effects of cumulative long-term pesticide exposure, which is linked to cancer and infertility, who cares about an eighty-five cent price difference? Really.

Produce:

Produce is the biggest concern because fresh fruits and vegetables are heavily sprayed with pesticides (agrochemicals) to ensure crop survival and are treated for transport. All produce should be washed well, even better scrubbed with a bristle brush. If the produce is not organic, always **wash and peel it** to reduce pesticide ingestion. Commercially grown berries and strawberries have over 60 pesticides on them, so you should always buy them organic. Same with spinach and leafy greens because they have systemic pesticides, meaning the pesticides were drawn up from the soil into the plant so there is no washing it off; it is inside your veg. You can, however, remove the skins from commercially

grown fruits and vegetables to reduce pesticide exposure. Yeah, this is how we manufacture food in America. Educate yourself. Do your own research and determine what is most feasible for you.

Remember, eating any produce is better than eating none at all! So enjoy all those wonderful fresh foods you have selected. No matter what!

Meat, Poultry, Fish, Eggs:

Proteins are the building blocks that the human body uses to form and repair organs, nerves, muscles, and flesh. Therefore, when buying animal proteins like meat, fish, and eggs, it is crucial to buy the best quality available. The way the animal led its life, what it was fed, how it was treated, and how it was slaughtered impacts the quality of the meat. The positives and negatives of that quality will be passed on directly to you.

Look for words like grass-fed, pasture-fed, free-range, cage free, local, organic, and antibiotic- or hormone-free.

I purchase all of my meats from the natural foods store and my local fishmonger. These stores tend to carry locally sourced meat and fish. I know my dollar will stay in the local economy, and it will most likely support a small farmer or fisherman. This is a commitment I have made to myself and to my community.

Meat should never be wasted. Every scrap should be made use of, whether it's scraps given to pets or bones boiled down for stock. Be thankful for the sacrifice and flesh of the animal whose life was taken for your sustenance. To let the meat rot in your fridge because you forgot about it is blatantly wrong and unconscionable.

On the Shopping Lists and in the Ingredients Guide, **I note with an asterisk (*) the items I personally make an effort to buy organic or best quality.** Again, do what is affordable for you. The way I see it, real food costs what it costs to plant, grow, pick, wash, deliver, and stock on your supermarket shelves. Don't be cheap with yourself. You are worth the extra cost. Besides, you are already saving tons of money by not eating every meal out this week.

PLU? Who Knew?

PRODUCE
94608

The PLU codes (price lookup numbers) on the stickers of produce tell you if the food was organically grown, produced with chemical fertilizers, fungicides, or herbicides, or genetically modified.

Remember these easy numbers and you'll do just fine.

PLU starting with:
  9 is fine = organically grown–no pesticides
  3 or 4 wash and peel before = commercially grown–with pesticides
  8 not on my plate! = GMO– genetically modified food

Important foods to buy organic/best quality:

*Apples and applesauce

*Berries

*Grapes

*Celery

*Cucumbers

*Salad greens

*Spinach

*Grape tomatoes

*Bell peppers

*Potatoes

*Meat, poultry, fish

*Eggs

Blue Week

AKA EXOTIC GETAWAY

MENU

Theme: Mediterranean/Middle Eastern
Prep Day Length: 2 hours
Total Meals for the Week: 60%

PREP DAY RECIPES
Quinoa, *p. 52*
Tzatziki, *p. 52*
Charbroiled Vegetables, *p. 54*
Hummus, *p. 56*
Mixed Salad, *p. 57*
Tabouleh, *p. 58*

BREAKFAST
Whole Grain Cereal with Berries and Nuts, *p. 59*
Warm Quinoa Cereal, *p. 59*
Greek Yogurt Bowl with Fruit, Nuts, and Honey, *p. 36*
Smoothies, *p. 124*

LUNCH
Mediterranean Salad with Oranges, *p. 60*
Greek Chicken Salad, *p. 60*
Leftovers from Dinner:
Mediterranean Meze Plate: Hummus, Tzatziki, Tabouleh, *p. 61*
Charbroiled Vegetable Lasagna

DINNER
Yogurt-Marinated Chicken Kebabs with Tzatziki, *p. 62*
Personal Pita Pizzas *(p. 64),* or Pasta Primavera *(p. 64)*
Grilled Veggie Pita Pocket with Hummus and Tabouleh, *p. 64*
Charbroiled Vegetable Lasagna, *p. 65*

EXTRAS
Pita Chips, *p. 66*
Steamed Summer Squash, *p. 67*
Tahini Tea Cookies with Orange Zest, *p. 68*
How to Open and Eat a Pomegranate, *p. 70*

PANTRY MUST-HAVES

Items and quantities needed for this entire Week. Do you have them?

**FLOUR,
PREFERABLY
WHOLE WHEAT**
1½ cups

**BAKING
POWDER**
¼ teaspoon

**VANILLA
EXTRACT**
1 tablespoon

SUGAR
¾ cup

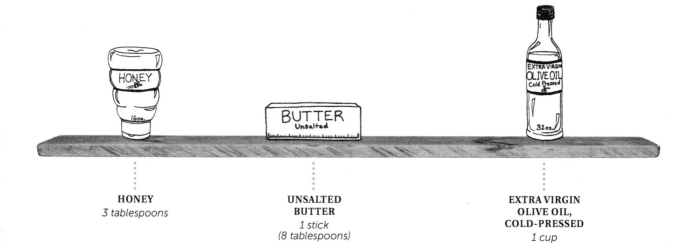

HONEY
3 tablespoons

**UNSALTED
BUTTER**
*1 stick
(8 tablespoons)*

**EXTRA VIRGIN
OLIVE OIL,
COLD-PRESSED**
1 cup

BASIL LEAVES, DRIED

CAYENNE PEPPER

CINNAMON, GROUND

OREGANO LEAVES, DRIED

PEPPER

RED PEPPER FLAKES

ROSEMARY LEAVES, DRIED

SAGE, GROUND

SALT

SMOKED PAPRIKA

THYME LEAVES, DRIED

TURMERIC

BLUE SHOPPING LIST

Read your labels! Make sure every item you put in your cart is
Food That Works approved. See page 18.

Fruit

Bananas: 4

Oranges: 2

Lemons: 2 to 3

Pomegranate: 1 (optional)

Vegetables

*Salad greens: 1 (5-ounce) tub, like organic spring mix

*Grape tomatoes: 1 pint

Garlic: 2 heads

Carrots: 1 (1-pound) bag

*Cucumbers: 2

Yellow onions: 2

Red onion: 1 small

*Green bell pepper: 1

*Red bell pepper: 1

Zucchini aka Italian squash: 2

Summer squash aka yellow squash: 2

Eggplant: 1 medium

Fresh Herbs

Mint: 1 bunch

Dill: 1 bunch

Basil: 1 bunch (optional)

Thyme: 1 bunch (optional)

Specialty Cheese Section

Sharp Cheddar cheese: 1 (10-ounce) block

Feta cheese: 1 (8- to 12-ounce) container best from bulk bar or deli

Kalamata olives: 1 container best from bulk bar or deli (optional)

Poultry

*Chicken breasts, boneless skinless: 1½ pounds

Baked Goods

Pitas, whole wheat, large: 1 package

Pasta, Grains, Nuts

Lasagna noodles, no-boil (aka oven-ready): 1 (8-ounce) box

Quinoa: 1 (12-ounce) package

Cereal of your choice, whole grain: 1 box, like Kashi Crunch

Almonds, whole, raw: 1 (1-pound) bag

Cans, Jars, Bottles & More

Chickpeas aka garbanzo beans: 1 (15-ounce) can

Beets, sliced: 1 (15-ounce) can (optional)

Spaghetti sauce: 1 (24-ounce) jar

Tahini sesame paste: 1 (10- to 16-ounce) jar

Sesame seeds: 1 small jar

Vanilla protein powder: 1 container (any size) (optional for Smoothies)

Wood or metal shish kebab skewers: 1 package (optional)

Refrigerated

Cottage cheese, country style small curd, plain: 1 (16-ounce) container

Greek yogurt, plain, full-fat: 1 (32-ounce) container

*Egg: 1 egg, if making tahini cookies (page 68)

Almond milk, unsweetened or milk of your choice: 1 (half gallon) carton

Frozen

*Blueberries: 1 (15-ounce) bag

Asterisk (*) suggests to buy organic

BLUE PREP DAY

NOW YOU HAVE ALL OF YOUR GROCERIES. With a little forethought, you will have fresh Mediterranean meals all week. This prep list is strategically designed to get you through this process efficiently; do as much as you can. Ready to multitask? Put on some music. Here we go! We are going to bust through this.

Decide what you want to make for dinner tonight. Keep in mind that after the prep work is completed, you may want something quick and easy.

Suggestion: Grilled Veggie Pita Pocket (page 64), with Hummus (page 56), and Tabouleh (page 58).

You will need: hand immersion blender, measuring cups, measuring spoons, large cutting board with a medium bowl next to it for scraps, chef's knife, vegetable peeler, grater, and containers and plastic bags to store chopped veggies.

Prep List:
1. Cook Quinoa
2. Cut lemons
3. Chop vegetables
4. Make Tzatziki
5. Make Hummus
6. Charbroil Vegetables
7. Assemble Tabouleh
8. Assemble Mixed Salad
9. Shred Cheddar cheese
   Cut extra summer squash (optional)
   Open pomegranate (optional)

1. Cook Quinoa:

Quinoa (page 52), allow to cool.

2. Cut lemons:

2 lemons—each cut into 6 wedges, 12 total. Place in a plastic bag and refrigerate. Use within 5 days.

3. Chop vegetables:

For definitions of chop, mince, zest, etc., see page 20.

Cucumbers:
2 cucumbers—peel; discard peels in the scrap bowl. Reserve half of 1 cucumber for Tzatziki recipe. Slice remaining cucumbers into ½-inch rounds. Place in a plastic bag with a splash of water to keep them moist, and refrigerate. Use for dips and to add to salads. Use within 5 days.

4. Make Tzatziki:

Tzatziki (page 52).

5. Make Hummus:

Hummus (page 56).

Chop vegetables continued...

Carrots:
4 carrots—scrub, rinse, dry, and slice carrots into snack-size sticks for Hummus. Place in a plastic bag with a splash of water to keep them moist, and refrigerate. You may want to divide the carrot sticks into serving-size bags for easy snacks on the go. Use within 7 days.

Onion:
1 red onion—finely chop and store in a container in the refrigerator. Use within 7 days.

6. Make Charbroiled Vegetables:

Charbroiled Vegetables (page 54).

7. Assemble Tabouleh:

Tabouleh (page 58).

9. Shred Cheddar cheese:

Shred half the block of cheese on the large holes of a grater (about 1½ cups) for quick access during the week. Store in the refrigerator in a plastic bag with the air removed. Use within 7 days.

Done! Your fridge should look awesome and organized.

....

Feeling ambitious?

You may have an extra half of a zucchini and a summer squash. Raw zucchini and summer squash have a great nutty flavor—try a piece.

Chop them up and add to Mixed Salad, or cut them into rounds to dip in Hummus.

Don't like them raw? Steam them one night for a nice side dish (page 67).

Open pomegranate (page 70).

....

Reuse your scraps!

Reduce the amount of trash and landfill waste you produce by repurposing the vegetable matter in your scrap bowl.

Feed Yourself: Toss your veggie scraps into a bag in the freezer and keep adding to it each week. Once it is full, use it to make a delicious broth.

Feed the Soil: Find a way to compost your veggie scraps and allow them to biodegrade naturally back into the earth.

8. Assemble Mixed Salad:

Mixed Salad (page 57).

PREP DAY RECIPES

Quinoa *(KEEN-wah)*

Total Time: 20 minutes · Makes: 4 ½ cups

Quinoa has been labeled a "super grain" because it has superior nutritional properties. This ancient grain has a light fluffy texture, nutty taste, and cooks faster than rice. The uses for quinoa are endless. It can be added to any dish, hot or cold, and used as a substitute for rice or pasta.

It is important to remove the bitter saponin, which is a natural glucose residue from the plant. If it is consumed in large amounts, it can upset the intestinal tract and cause diarrhea. To remove the saponin, the quinoa must be washed thoroughly before cooking by placing it in water, and rubbing it between your fingers, giving it a good "scrub." Rinse and repeat several times until the water runs clear.

1 teaspoon salt
1½ cups washed quinoa

Stove Top:

In a medium pot with a lid, add 2¾ cups cold water and the salt. Place over medium-high heat; bring to a boil, about 5 minutes.

Place the washed quinoa in the boiling water and cover.

Reduce the heat to low. Simmer about 15 minutes; set timer.

Quinoa is done when it is tender to the bite, light, and fluffy. If quinoa is done, but the water is not fully absorbed, remedy this by draining off the excess water and fluffing the quinoa with a fork over low heat for a few seconds to dry it out.

Tip

With any grain you are cooking (rice, quinoa, barley), you always want to wash it first. Not only does this remove those belly-irritating starches mentioned above, but by washing/scrubbing, you remove pesticide residues, like arsenic, which is most prevalent on rice, especially on brown rice, because it still has all of its casing.

Remove from the heat, fluff again, and allow to cool, uncovered.

Transfer to a container, store in the refrigerator, and use in meals throughout the week.

Rice Cooker:

Place the washed quinoa in a rice cooker.

Add 2¾ cups cold water and the salt. Cover; press start on the rice cooker.

Once done, remove from the cooker, fluff with fork, and allow to cool uncovered.

Use in:

Tabouleh
Hummus
Warm Quinoa Cereal
Mediterranean Salad
Grilled Veggie Pita Pocket

Tzatziki *(tsaht-ZEE-kee)* Greek Cucumber Garlic Yogurt Dip

Total Time: 20 minutes · Makes: 2 cups

This dip rules. It not only tastes great, but it's also great for you. Greek yogurt is full of probiotics, which aid the gut in healthy digestion. Olive oil supports healthy heart function. Fresh herbs and raw garlic are antifungal, full of vitamins, and boost your immune system. Along with a dose of vitamin C from fresh-squeezed lemon juice, this Tzatziki is a nutritional powerhouse.

Heap tzatziki on top of your salad instead of a creamy dressing or use it as a dip. Do as they do in the Middle East and the Mediterranean and make a meze plate, a meal of small plates, dips, and salads (page 61).

1 tablespoon extra virgin olive oil
Juice from 2 lemon wedges (⅓ lemon)
1 cup plain full-fat Greek yogurt
5-6 cloves of garlic, finely chopped
½ peeled cucumber, shredded on the large holes of a grater
¼ cup chopped fresh mint leaves
¼ cup chopped fresh dill weed
¼ teaspoon salt

In a medium bowl, combine olive oil and lemon juice; whisk well until cloudy.

Add the yogurt, making sure to mix fully so it does not curdle. (If yogurt curdles from the lemon, it is not rancid or bad, it just doesn't look very pretty. It tastes fine and is perfectly safe to eat)

Stir in the garlic, cucumber, mint, dill, and salt. Taste and adjust seasonings to your liking.

This dip is best after it is refrigerated overnight. The taste is enhanced with time. Store, covered, in the refrigerator; use within 7 days.

Use in:

Mediterranean Salad

Greek Chicken Salad

Mediterranean Meze Plate

Yogurt-Marinated Chicken Kebab

WARNING

Tzatziki is very garlic forward. This is what I love about it. If you are not a garlic lover, use only 3 cloves and add extra mint and dill.

Charbroiled Vegetables

Total Time: 25 minutes · Makes: 4 cups

Broiling means to cook under extremely high heat, around 500°F, very close to the heat source. Food gets cooked within minutes and gets that blackened, charred flavor as if it were cooked on an outdoor grill. Food broils *extremely quickly,* so it is important that you set timers, check it often as it cooks, and do not walk away! Always leave the oven door ajar while broiling. For more instructions on broiling, see page 22.

Don't fuss on the exact size you chop the veggies; they will be equally delicious no matter how you cut them!

- **1 green bell pepper, stems, core, and seeds removed, cut into 1-inch pieces**
- **1 zucchini, sliced into ½-inch rounds**
- **1 summer squash, sliced into ½-inch rounds**
- **3 tablespoons extra virgin olive oil, divided**
- **Salt**
- **Pepper**
- **½ teaspoon dried oregano**
- **½ teaspoon red pepper flakes**
- **1 large pinch dried or fresh rosemary**
- **1 medium eggplant, sliced into ½-inch rounds**
- **1 yellow onion, sliced into ½-inch rounds—try to keep rounds intact**

Preheat oven to Broil–High. Position the top rack as high as possible so that the veggies are about 2 inches from the heat source. Line a large baking sheet with tin foil.

Place the green peppers, zucchini, and squash in a large bowl. Add 1 tablespoon olive oil, ½ teaspoon salt, ½ teaspoon pepper, oregano, red pepper flakes, and rosemary. Toss with your hands or a spoon to evenly coat veggies.

Spread the veggies in a single layer on the prepared baking sheet. Depending on the size of your baking sheet, you may need to broil these in batches. Place the peppers skin-side up so they blacken nicely. Remember the highest points are going to char first and *fast!*

Place the baking sheet on the top rack of the oven; set timer for 5 minutes, watch closely. Broil the veggies, checking on them often, until they are well charred (blackened) and the peppers are soft, about 5 minutes.

Transfer to a plate to cool. Resist eating them all!

Lay out the eggplants and onions in one layer on the same tin foil used for the veggies.

Pour the remaining 2 tablespoons olive oil in a small bowl. Dip your fingers into the oil and massage the front and back of each eggplant and onion slice. The eggplant will try to suck up the oil, but you don't need much. Try to keep the onion rings intact.

Lay them flat on the baking sheet. Generously season with salt and pepper.

Broil:

Place the baking sheet on the top rack of the oven; set timer for 5 minutes, watch closely. Broil the eggplant and onions, checking on them often, until they are well charred.

Place all broiled veggies together on a plate to cool. Cover with plastic wrap or tin foil and refrigerate.

Use in:

Grilled Veggie Pita Pocket
Charbroiled Vegetable Lasagna

Tip

If your oven's highest rack is not quite close enough to the heat source, you will not receive the desired char effect. You want veggies to be 1 to 2 inches away from the heat source. To get your vegetables closer to the heat, place a second baking sheet or shallow baking dish flipped face down on the top rack. Then slide your vegetable-filled baking sheet on top of that to raise the veggies a few inches.

Hummus

Total Time: 20 minutes
Makes: 2 cups, 3 cups with Quinoa

Once you make fresh hummus, you won't want to return to that expensive store-bought stuff that's filled with preservatives. By making it yourself, you can add additional flavors like a large handful of chopped red peppers, cayenne pepper, chipotle peppers, pitted olives, sundried tomatoes, anchovies, capers, feta, pesto, extra garlic, or fresh herbs like parsley or basil. You live only once–experiment a little.

Depending on what I am using it for, I will make it creamy and thin or dense and thick. I'll even lighten it up by adding a cup of cooked quinoa, which gives hummus a fluffier texture, leaving me feeling less full and less weighed down. Adding quinoa will not only yield more hummus, but it makes each serving a little lower in calories and fat. If chickpeas upset your stomach, substitute any canned white bean. Chickpeas, beans, and quinoa are full of protein; tahini and olive oil have good fats; and lemon, garlic, and herbs all boost your immune system. Eat up!

Enjoy your hummus with Pita Chips (page 66), carrot sticks, sliced cucumbers, or any other raw veggies of your choice.

You will need a hand immersion blender, food processor or blender.

1 (15-ounce) can chickpeas, rinsed well and drained

5 tablespoons tahini, stir well before measuring (it tends to separate)

3-5 cloves garlic, whole

Juice from 4-5 lemon wedges ($^2/_3$ to $^5/_6$ lemon)

2 tablespoons extra virgin olive oil, plus more for garnish

½ teaspoon salt

1 dash dried oregano

1 dash paprika, plus more for garnish

1 dash turmeric, plus more for garnish

1 dash cayenne, plus more for garnish

¾ cup Quinoa (from Prep Day page 52) (optional)

Place the chickpeas in a deep bowl. Add the tahini, garlic, lemon juice, 5 to 6 tablespoons water, olive oil, salt, oregano, paprika, turmeric, cayenne, and quinoa (if using).

Puree with a hand immersion blender directly in the bowl. Keep the hand immersion blender submerged in contents to avoid splattering everywhere. Press hummus up against the sides of the bowl to extrude through the blade until completely smooth. Make sure garlic cloves got pureed. If you do not have a hand immersion blender, puree all ingredients in a food processor or blender until smooth.

Taste, and if needed, add more spices, salt, or lemon. Add additional ingredients if you like; puree again.

If too thick, add small amounts of water until the hummus is the desired consistency.

Remember, as it chills, flavors will change and intensify, especially the lemon. If you think it needs more lemon now, add a little lemon zest. That gives you lemon essence without the acid.

Mound the hummus in a bowl or a container. Smooth out the top with the back of a spoon and garnish with a drizzle of olive oil, pinches of paprika, oregano, and turmeric to decorate it with dashes of color.

Since this hummus is fresh, it does not contain preservatives. Keep covered and refrigerated. Use within 6 days.

Use in:

Mediterranean Salad
Mediterranean Meze Plate
Grilled Veggie Pita Pocket

Tip

Can't eat it all? Hummus freezes well. Place in a container, leaving at least ½ inch of space at the top for expansion. Bang the container a few times on the countertop to pack down the hummus and remove any air pockets. Cover hummus with a thin layer of olive oil; this creates a barrier so the moisture from the hummus doesn't leach out. Cover tightly, label, and freeze up to four months. When you want to eat it, just defrost it in the fridge for about a day. Stir, taste, and add additional spices if you like.

Mixed Salad Blue Week

Total Time: 3 minutes

Assemble this colorful salad on your Prep Day for easy grabbing throughout the week. Don't even think about it; just dump the ingredients directly into the plastic tub that the salad greens came in. *Voilà!* Your fridge is now a salad bar. This Mixed Salad will serve as a dry base to build upon with toppings and leftovers. To-go meals can be assembled in minutes and then you are out the door!

This Mixed Salad is deliberately composed of dryish vegetables so that it will last for 7 days in the refrigerator. "Dry" ingredients will not cause the lettuce to wilt prematurely. This is why you don't halve the tomatoes now or add "wet" ingredients like peppers or cucumber.

Mixed Salad:

1 (5-ounce) tub salad greens
½ pint grape tomatoes, rinsed and dried
2 carrots, scrubbed, rinsed, dried, and sliced into thin rounds

Open the tub of salad greens.
Dump the tomatoes and carrots directly into the Mixed Salad container. Toss lightly with your hands.
Keep covered and refrigerated. Use within 7 days.

Throughout the week, top individual servings of Mixed Salad with the toppings of your choice: Leftovers, cottage cheese, salsa, hummus, chopped veggies, fresh herbs, chopped apples, orange segments, grapes, raisins, nuts, seeds, cheese, olives, canned beans, hard-boiled eggs, cooked grains, chicken or fish.

When I found out that baby carrots are just big carrot nubs whittled down on machines, I stopped buying them. The whittling process is not only weird, but you lose out on the majority of nutrients located in the first layer of skin. Aren't nutrients the entire point of eating carrots?

The skin on vegetables is what preserves them. When this natural preservative is removed, like in peeled baby carrots, it must be replaced with a preservative, like nitrogen, which is what they spray in the bag to increase shelf life.

Do the big-kid thing, and buy a bag of full-size carrots, scrub them, and chop them up yourself.

PREP DAY RECIPE

Tabouleh *(tuh-boo-lee)*

Total Time: 15 minutes · Makes: 3 cups

This Middle Eastern salad has incredible flavor and is a delicious option in the hot summer months. Traditionally, Tabouleh is made with bulgar, but I use quinoa.

    2 cups Quinoa (from Prep Day page 52)
    ½ cup finely chopped fresh mint leaves
    ½ pint grape tomatoes, cut in quarters
    ½ cup crumbled feta
    ¼ cup chopped red onions
    1 tablespoon extra virgin olive oil
    ¼ teaspoon salt
    2-3 lemon wedges (⅓ to ½ lemon)

Combine the quinoa, mint, tomatoes, feta, onions, olive oil, and salt in a medium bowl. Squeeze the lemon juice on top. Stir gently to combine. Taste, and add more of any ingredient until it tastes good to you.

Place the tabouleh in a covered container and refrigerate; use within 7 days. Flavors get better over time.

Use in:

Mediterranean Meze Plate
Yogurt-Marinated Chicken Kebab

Tip

Extra mint leaves? Make mint tea! Tear up 6 mint leaves and toss into a mug of hot water. Allow to steep a few minutes then remove. Add sweetener if desired. Fresh mint has medicinal properties. Not only is it calming, but it also soothes indigestion and relieves nausea and congestion.

Whole Grain Cereal with Berries and Nuts

Total Time: 5 minutes · Serves: 1

I rarely buy boxed cereal, but once in a while, it is a quick breakfast I must resort to. Cereal must be thought of as a garnish to the rest of your breakfast. A serving size of cereal is a measly ¾ to 1 cup; and a serving of milk is 1 cup. There is no way that will hold me long enough to get through my commute without killing people. So I add fruit and nuts to my cereal, or I skip the milk and serve it all atop a serving of Greek yogurt for a more hearty breakfast. Again, protein in the morning will keep you full–and civil. Or enjoy a small serving of cereal and then get your protein in on the side with a smoothie, a hard-boiled egg, or a rice cake with almond butter.

1 cup almond milk, or plain full-fat Greek yogurt
1 cup whole grain cereal
½ cup frozen blueberries or ½ banana, sliced
¼ cup nuts

Combine the almond milk, cereal, fruit, and nuts in a bowl.

Tip

Select cereal that has "100% whole grain" as the first listed ingredient and is both high in protein (6 grams or more) and low in sugar (15 grams or less). I recommend Kashi GOLEAN Crunch varieties because they meet these requirements. Most boxed cereals are high in sugar and simple carbs, which leave you with a mid-morning energy crash and will not keep you satiated until lunch. Therefore, it's important to read the ingredients label on boxed cereal *while you are at the store*. We all know, once it's in the house, it's too late!

Try my morning tonic: In a mug of hot water, add a few dashes of ground turmeric, honey, a tablespoon of apple cider vinegar, and juice from half a lemon. Ziiing! You will be skippin' into the office!

Warm Quinoa Cereal

Total Time: 5 minutes · Serves: 1

Adding quinoa to your morning oatmeal gives it a new complex nutty flavor, stretches those instant oats further, and provides you with a big hearty bowl to dig in to. Quinoa is loaded with fiber and protein to ensure you are full and fueled to start your day.

Not a fan of the texture of oatmeal? You can forego the oats altogether in this recipe and just heat up quinoa with almond milk, cinnamon, sweetener, nuts, and any other toppings of your choice.

1 cup Quinoa (from Prep Day page 52)
½ cup almond milk or milk of your choice
¼ cup instant oats (if you have them)
Generous dashes of cinnamon
2 teaspoons sweetener of your choice (honey, maple syrup or brown sugar)
¼ cup whole almonds
Optional Toppings: blueberries, raisins, fresh fruit, fruit preserves, shredded coconut, etc.

Stovetop:

In a small pot, stir together the quinoa, almond milk, and oats.

Cook over medium-high heat until hot. Stir occasionally so it does not stick to the bottom. Once it begins to bubble, remove from heat.

Add the cinnamon, sweetener, and almonds. Stir and taste. If necessary, add more almond milk to reach desired thickness.

Tip

Combine these ingredients in a bowl the night before, cover with plastic wrap, and refrigerate. Microwave it in the morning. Really can't mess this one up.

Microwave:

Place the quinoa, almond milk, and oats in a bowl; stir.

Heat in a microwave 2 to 3 minutes.

Add the cinnamon, sweetener, and almonds. Stir and taste. If quinoa is too thick, add more almond milk to reach desired thickness.

Load on your favorite toppings.

LUNCH

Mediterranean Salad with Oranges

Total Time: 15 minutes · Serves: 2

I could eat this salad every day of my life. Fruit in my salad is one of my favorite things; I love the combination of sweet fruit and crunchy vegetables. This salad is a great way to use up any leftover ingredients in your fridge at the end of the week. If you have the time, and like tahini, try the Orange Tahini Dressing.

1 cup Quinoa (from Prep Day page 52) or Tabouleh (from Prep Day page 58)
½ cup sliced cucumber
1 orange, peeled, seeded, and chopped
1 (15-ounce) can sliced beets, rinsed and drained (optional)
½ cup crumbled feta
1 cup pomegranate seeds (optional)
Optional Toppings: 1 teaspoon sesame seeds, 4 torn mint leaves, torn fresh dill, or hummus
Extra virgin olive oil
Salt
Pepper
2 large handfuls Mixed Salad
½ cup whole almonds
2 lemon wedges (⅓ lemon)

If you are taking this salad to go, start by putting the dressing and wet ingredients at the bottom of the container so that they don't make the rest of the salad soggy.

Divide the Quinoa, cucumber, oranges, beets, and feta into two separate to-go containers. Add optional toppings if you like. Drizzle olive oil over salads; season with salt and pepper. Top with Mixed Salad, then the almonds. Toss in the lemon wedges. Cover and refrigerate.

Before eating, squeeze juice from the lemon wedge over the salad. Replace the cover, and shake vigorously to toss the salad well and combine the flavors.

Orange Tahini Dressing
(optional)

Prep Time: 5 minutes · Serves: 2

Can't get enough of that tahini? Make it into a dressing. Instead of the savory kick of garlic that tahini is usually paired with, this dressing highlights tahini's sweet side with orange juice and orange zest. Use this tasty dressing with carrots, on salads, drizzled on steamed cauliflower or cold beets and feta. For instructions on how to zest, see page 20.

2 teaspoons orange zest (from about half the orange)
Juice from 1 orange
1 tablespoon extra virgin olive oil
2 tablespoons tahini
1 teaspoon plain full-fat Greek yogurt

Combine the zest, juice, olive oil, tahini, and yogurt in a bowl. Whisk together well. Store in a glass jar in the refrigerator. Use within 7 days.

Greek Chicken Salad

Total Time: 15 minutes · Serves: 2

Arrange the leftover ingredients from chicken kebabs on top of a salad for a quick lunch. Now you get to enjoy that awesome meal twice! *Opa!*

Generous spoonfuls of Tzatziki (page 52) instead of dressing
½ cup chopped red onions
½ cup sliced cucumber
Leftover cooked chicken from Kebabs (page 62)
½ cup crumbled feta
Optional Toppings: Kalamata olives; capers; and canned chickpeas, rinsed well and drained
Extra virgin olive oil
Dried oregano
Salt
Pepper
2 large handfuls Mixed Salad
2 lemon wedges (⅓ lemon)

If you are taking this salad to go, start by putting the dressing and wet ingredients at the bottom of the container so that they don't make the rest of the salad soggy.

Divide the Tzatziki, onions, cucumbers, chicken, and feta into two separate to-go containers. Add optional toppings if you like. Drizzle olive oil over salads; season with oregano, salt and pepper. Top with Mixed Salad. Toss in the lemon wedges. Cover and refrigerate.

Before eating, squeeze juice from the lemon wedge over the salad. Replace the cover, and shake vigorously to toss the salad well and combine the flavors.

Mediterranean Meze (meh-ZAY) Plate

Total Time: 15 minutes · Serves: 1

In the Middle East and the Mediterranean, "*meze*" refers to a combination of small plates including dips, salads, nuts, olives, and cheeses. Spaniards would call them "*tapas*," Turks would say "*meze*," and Greeks "*mezedes*." This popular appetizer is typically presented on a big platter and shared among friends. With all of the Mediterranean delights you prepared on your Prep Day, this gorgeous meze spread can be assembled in minutes. Below are just some guidelines to create your own *personal* meze plate. Make it pretty!

½ cup Tzatziki (from Prep Day page 52)
½ cup Hummus (from Prep Day page 56)
½ cup Tabouleh (from Prep Day page 58) or
    Quinoa (from Prep Day page 52)
Small amounts of sliced cucumbers, carrot
    sticks, sliced pita, feta, olives, almonds
1 lemon wedge (⅙ lemon)
Extra virgin olive oil
Dried oregano
Salt

Arrange beautiful piles of the dips, vegetables, pita, feta, olives, nuts, and quinoa on a plate. Use whatever you've got in the fridge! There are no rules.

Finish with a squeeze of lemon juice and a drizzle of olive oil. Sprinkle some oregano and salt on top.

DINNER

Yogurt-Marinated Chicken Kebabs with Tzatziki

Prep Time: 25 minutes · Cook Time: 15 minutes
Serves: 4

I am pretty sure I had at least one kebab every day for the ninety days I lived in Turkey. Although kebabs differ on every corner, this is my attempt at a Turkish-inspired kebab plate. Marinating the chicken in yogurt not only makes it tender and moist, but also gives it a nice tangy, exotic flavor. This dish will have your guests inquiring what you added to make the kebabs so moist and zippy!

For more instructions on broiling, see page 22.

Marinade:

¼ cup extra virgin olive oil
Juice from 2-3 lemon wedges (⅓ to ½ lemon)
½ cup plain full-fat Greek yogurt
6 cloves garlic, finely chopped
2 teaspoons dried thyme
2 teaspoons dried oregano
1 teaspoon salt
1 teaspoon pepper
½ teaspoon smoked paprika
¼ teaspoon cayenne pepper
¼ teaspoon red pepper flakes

Kebabs:

1½ pounds skinless, boneless chicken breasts, trimmed of fat, cut in 1½-inch cubes
1 red bell pepper, stem, core, and seeds removed, cut into 1½-inch pieces
1 yellow onion, peeled, cut into 1½-inch pieces, try to keep intact for skewers
2 teaspoons extra virgin olive oil
Salt
Pepper

Serve with:

Tabouleh (from Prep Day page 58)
Tzatziki (from Prep Day page 52)
Mixed Salad (from Prep Day page 57)
Whole wheat pitas (optional)

Soak 6 wood skewers in water for at least 20 minutes to prevent them from burning.

Marinade:

In a medium bowl, combine the olive oil and lemon juice; whisk well until cloudy.

Add the yogurt, making sure to whisk well so it does not curdle. (If yogurt curdles from the lemon, it is not rancid or bad, it just doesn't look very pretty. The taste will be fine and it is perfectly safe to eat.)

Add the garlic, thyme, oregano, salt, pepper, smoked paprika, cayenne, and red pepper flakes; mix well.

Place the cubed chicken in a sturdy plastic bag. Pour the marinade into the bag. Remove the air, seal the bag, and massage the outside of the bag with your hands, coating all the chicken pieces with the marinade. Place in the refrigerator for at least 30 minutes or even overnight.

When ready to make the meal:

Preheat oven to Broil–High. Position the top rack as high as possible so that the skewers are about 2 inches from the heat source. Line a large baking sheet with tin foil.

Using a pastry brush or your hands, massage the peppers and onions with a little olive oil, place on the prepared baking sheet.

Skewers:

If using skewers, thread the chicken, peppers, and onions on each one. Place on the prepared baking sheet. Discard the rest of the marinade.

No Skewers:

If not using skewers, spread the peppers and onions in a single layer on one side of the prepared baking sheet, and spread the marinated chicken on the other. Discard the rest of marinade.

Generously season with salt and pepper.

Broil the skewers on the top rack of the oven until the chicken is cooked through and veggies are charred. Set timer for 10 to 15 minutes to check for doneness. You can turn the skewers or flip the chicken and veggies once, if needed. Slice one piece of chicken open to check if it is cooked through. Middle should be juicy, yet white all the way through. If you see any pink, cook longer.

Plate the Tabouleh, Tzatziki, and Mixed Salad. Place the chicken kebabs on top. Serve pitas on the side.

Tip
Instead of serving this as a kebab plate, you can tuck all these ingredients into a pita pocket!

LEFTOVERS:
Use leftovers in Greek Chicken Salad (page 60). You will be so happy you get to enjoy this meal again tomorrow! OH MY!

Personal Pita Pizzas

Total Time: 20 minutes · Serves: 2

Here is a quick and tasty meal to use up those pitas, spare veggies, and that jarred spaghetti sauce. The pita is your crust, go forth and decorate. You know the drill.

2 large whole wheat pitas
½ cup jarred spaghetti sauce, plus more for dipping
1 cup shredded cheese
½ cup chopped red onions
½ cup thinly sliced zucchini
½ cup thinly sliced summer squash
Optional Toppings: feta, olives, capers, bell peppers, fresh herbs, fennel seeds, leftover charbroiled vegetables
Extra virgin olive oil
Dried oregano
Dried sage
Red pepper flakes
Salt

Preheat oven to Bake 400°F. Position a rack in the middle of the oven. Line a large baking sheet with tin foil.

Place the pitas on the prepared baking sheet and bake them for 5 minutes to ensure a crispy crust.

Remove the pan from the oven. Spread spaghetti sauce on each pita using a spoon; sprinkle with handfuls of cheese. Load the pitas up with veggies and any other toppings you can find. Drizzle lightly with olive oil. Sprinkle with generous amounts of oregano, sage, red pepper flakes, and salt.

Return the pan to the oven, and bake until the cheese is fully melted and golden. Set timer for 10 to 15 minutes; keep checking until done.

Serve with a side of Mixed Salad and extra spaghetti sauce for dipping. I prefer hot sauce!

Tip: These pizzas freeze wonderfully! Allow to cool completely on a wire rack. Wrap tightly in tin foil, and then seal in a plastic bag, label, and freeze. Reheat frozen pizzas in the oven on a lazy night.

Grilled Veggie Pita Pocket with Hummus and Tabouleh

Total Time: 15 minutes · Serves: 2

I frequent this recipe when I find myself longing for summer. This delicious pita, stuffed with blackened veggies, tahini, and feta is light yet so satisfying. Wrap it in plastic wrap or tin foil for a transportable lunch and all your coworkers will be asking, "Where did you buy that?" (Wink)

If you did not broil veggies in advance, it takes about 25 minutes. Follow the Charbroiled Vegetables Recipe (page 54).

1 large whole wheat pita
½ cup Hummus (from Prep Day page 56)
½ cup crumbled feta
½ cup Quinoa (from Prep Day page 52) (optional)
1½ cups Charbroiled Vegetables (from Prep Day page 54)

Tahini Sauce (optional)

4 tablespoons tahini
Juice from 3 lemon wedges (½ lemon)
1 tablespoon extra virgin olive oil
2 cups Tabouleh (from Prep Day page 58)

Cut the pita in half to form two pockets. Gently open them.

Divide the ingredients between the two pita pockets. Spread Hummus in the pockets, add feta and quinoa. Stuff with as many charbroiled veggies as you like.

Tahini Sauce:

Whisk the tahini, lemon juice, and oil together in a bowl, or combine them in a glass jar and shake vigorously. Drizzle the sauce into the pita pocket.

Serve with a side of Tabouleh.

Tip

Like it hot? Preheat oven to 350°F. Stuff the pita, wrap loosely in tin foil, place on the oven rack. Bake for 10 minutes.

Charbroiled Vegetable Lasagna

Prep Time: 30 minutes · Cook Time: 45 minutes
Serves: 4

Applying *Food That Works* principles to old favorites like lasagna will expedite the preparation and improve your health. Use "no-boil" or "oven-ready" pasta to cut down prep time. Then use red sauce instead of olive oil to coat the pan. Try cottage cheese in place of ricotta to cut the calories in half and the fat to a fourth! Lastly, delicious charbroiled vegetables are a hearty, flavorful replacement for beef. Serve this lasagna with a side salad for an exceptionally colorful plate.

If you did not broil veggies in advance, it takes about 25 minutes. Follow the Charbroiled Vegetables Recipe (page 54).

- 4 cloves garlic, minced
- 1 tablespoon dried oregano, plus more for sprinkling (fresh herbs are better)
- 1 tablespoon dried basil (fresh herbs are better)
- ½ teaspoon dried rosemary (fresh herbs are better)
- ½ teaspoon dried sage (fresh herbs are better)
- ½ teaspoon salt, plus more for sprinkling
- ¼ teaspoon black pepper
- 1 (16-ounce) container country style plain cottage cheese
- 1½ cups jarred spaghetti sauce
- 1 (8-ounce) box no-boil lasagna noodles
- 2½-3 cups Charbroiled Vegetables (from Prep Day page 54)
- ½ cup shredded sharp Cheddar cheese
- Red pepper flakes
- Chopped fresh basil leaves (if you have them)

Preheat oven to Bake 400°F. Position a rack in the middle of the oven.

Choose a baking dish for this small lasagna, an 8-inch square, 11- by 7-inch, or two 8- by 4-inch loaf pans will do.

To avoid dirtying a bowl, stir the garlic, oregano, basil, rosemary, sage, salt, and pepper directly into the cottage cheese in its container. Taste, adjust seasonings to your liking. This is the filling for your lasagna, so don't be shy, really pile on those spices! Leave the spoon in the mixture, and set aside.

Place the spaghetti sauce in a small bowl.

Place two heaping spoonfuls of sauce in the bottom of the baking dish or loaf pans. Tip the dish to spread the sauce along the sides, basically greasing the pan with sauce so the lasagna doesn't stick.

Add a layer of lasagna noodles, snapping them into the shapes needed to cover the bottom of the pan. Make sure they do not overlap.

Spread a thin layer of sauce on the noodles.

Arrange about one-third of the roasted veggies on top; overlapping is fine.

Spoon on a few dollops of the cottage cheese mixture, and spread it over the veggies.

Repeat layers two more times.

Top with a single layer of noodles.

Finish with sauce and top with cheese. Sprinkle with oregano, salt, red pepper flakes, and fresh basil.

Cover the lasagna with tin foil, and bake 30 minutes.

Remove the foil and continue to bake until the lasagna is bubbling and the top is golden brown, another 15 to 20 minutes.

Insert a knife to make sure noodles are cooked and tender.

Let the lasagna rest for 15 minutes before cutting and serving.

Serve with a side of Mixed Salad.

Next time you make this, Call me!

EXTRAS

Pita Chips

Total Time: 20 minutes · Serves: 2
(1 large pita = 16 chips)

Baked pita chips are a more healthful option than fried chips, which are high in calories and fat. These chips are shockingly easy to make and have an awesome crunch. They are great with any of the dips you are making this week (Hummus or Tzatziki). You can flavor these chips any way you wish. By varying the herbs and spices, you can make them different every time, savory or even sweet!

Basic Chips:
1 large whole wheat pita
1 teaspoon extra virgin olive oil
1 pinch salt

Flavor variations to play with:

- Mexican chips–lime juice, ground cumin, cayenne pepper, and oregano
- Middle Eastern chips–chopped garlic, fresh herbs, and smoked paprika
- Dessert chips–cinnamon and sugar

Preheat oven to Bake 350°F. Position a rack in the middle of the oven. Line a large baking sheet with tin foil.

Lightly drizzle both sides of a pita with olive oil, spread it with a pastry brush or your hands, and lightly sprinkle with salt.

Add additional spices if you like.

On a cutting board, cut the pita into 8 wedges.

Tear the wedges apart at the seams to separate into chips.

Place on the prepared baking sheet.

Bake until golden, about 15 minutes. Enjoy hot or store in a bag and use within 5 days.

Tip

Not all salt is created equal. Whenever possible, select products that list "sea salt" rather than "salt" in the listed ingredients. Table salt is highly refined. Due to this industrial processing, the salt is stripped of its natural magnesium and trace minerals. It is then iodized and bleached before it hits your table. I state simply "salt" throughout this book; as always, do what works best for you.

Steamed Summer Squash

Total Time: 15 minutes · Serves: 1

I never had zucchini or summer squash until I was 18. My friend prepared it this way, and it immediately became my new favorite. Steaming is believed to be the most healthful cooking method as it maintains the most nutrients and flavor. Steamed vegetables are lovely things to have on hand in your fridge. If they are already cooked, you are more apt to add them to whatever it is you are eating, warm or cold. Toss them into a salad, omelet, pasta, or, as in this recipe, simply dressed with butter, lemon, and red pepper flakes.

Remember, this same procedure can be applied to any vegetable, and in any quantity you can fit in a pot with a lid! Full steam ahead!

For more information on steaming, see page 22.

Sliced zucchini
Sliced summer squash
1 dash dried rosemary
1 tablespoon unsalted butter
Juice from 1 lemon wedge (⅙ lemon)
1 dash red pepper flakes
Salt
Pepper

If you have a steamer basket:

Fill the base of a large pot with 1 inch of water. Insert steamer basket into the pot.

Place over medium-high heat.

Once steam rises off the water, add the zucchini and summer squash to the steamer basket. Add the rosemary. Cover, and set timer for 5 minutes. Test one slice for doneness. Should be bright in color, soft to the bite but not overcooked to the point of being mushy. The squash will continue to cook a little after being removed from the pot, so aim for undercooking them a little.

Once done, plate them. Add the butter, lemon juice, red pepper flakes, and salt and pepper to taste.

No steamer basket? No problem.

Place a pot with a lid over medium-high heat. Add a small amount of water to just cover the bottom, about ½ cup. Place the vegetables directly in the water; you can stack them on top of each other. The bottom pieces will boil a bit since they are touching the water but the others will steam. No big deal. Cover with the lid and set timer for 5 minutes. Then follow the rest of the directions above.

Tahini Tea Cookies with Orange Zest

EXTRAS

Prep Time: 15 minutes · Cook Time: 15 minutes
Makes: 26 cookies

This is my original creation inspired by a Turkish tahini pastry I *never forgot*. These are not chewy cookies; they are similar to tea biscuits, which I LOVE. Depending on what I found in my cupboard, I have topped these cookies in a variety of ways, sesame seeds being my favorite. Crushed pistachios, fig jam, or a chocolate chip pressed in the middle of each, I imagine, would also taste pretty good.

- 4 tablespoons (½ stick) unsalted butter, at room temperature
- ½ cup sugar
- 2 teaspoons orange zest (from about half of 1 orange)
- ¾ cup tahini, stir well before measuring
- 1 egg
- ½ teaspoon vanilla extract
- 1 cup flour
- ¼ teaspoon baking powder
- 2 tablespoons sesame seeds

Preheat oven to Bake 350°F. Position a rack in the middle of the oven. Line a large baking sheet with parchment paper.

In a medium bowl, combine softened butter, sugar, and zest.

Mash the mixture up against the sides of the bowl with the back of a large spoon to blend the butter and sugar into small crumbly pieces.

Add the tahini, stir, and mash into a well-mixed paste.

Add the egg and vanilla; mix well until it is the consistency of peanut butter. A few small butter chunks are okay.

Add the flour and baking powder, and mix fully. Dough should be dry enough to handle and roll into balls.

Roll 1 tablespoon of dough at a time between your palms, a little smaller than golf balls.

Pour the sesame seeds into a small bowl, and roll the balls in the sesame seeds to coat.

Place the balls on the prepared baking sheet, and press with the back of a spoon to flatten them to equal thickness so they cook evenly.

Bake until the edges turn light golden brown, 15 to 18 minutes. Set timer.

Cool on a wire rack; transfer to MOUTH!

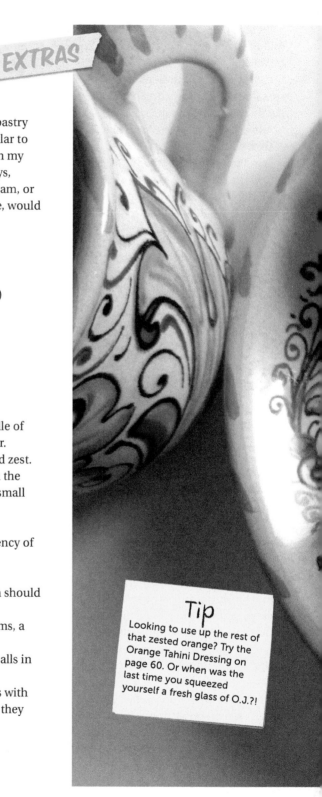

Tip

Looking to use up the rest of that zested orange? Try the Orange Tahini Dressing on page 60. Or when was the last time you squeezed yourself a fresh glass of O.J.?!

How to Open and Eat a Pomegranate

Total Time: 5 minutes

WHILE LIVING IN a small village in southern Turkey, I often saw Turkish women sitting outside working hard beating something with the back of a wooden spoon. I had no idea what they were doing until I asked one day and learned that they were striking the backs of halved pomegranates. I watched as the seeds effortlessly showered out into the bowl beneath. I had to laugh to myself for all the frustrating time I had spent in my kitchen trying, quite unsuccessfully, to pry the juicy ruby-like seeds out by hand. Here is the easiest way to get seeds out of a pomegranate; I had to share it.

This beautiful fruit has been revered as a symbol of health, fertility, and eternal life. Full of antioxidants, it is great for heart and blood vessel health, lowers blood pressure, promotes cell repair, and has antiaging properties. My two favorite ways of enjoying these beautiful rubies are in a salad for a crunchy sweet burst of flavor or on top of yogurt with a drizzle of honey to satisfy that late night sweet tooth. Who knew dessert could be so decadent *and* healthful?

1 pomegranate

Gently score the skin around the circumference of the pomegranate. Try not to cut through to the seeds or it gets messy.

Insert two thumbs near the incision, and crack the fruit open, in half.

Place a large deep bowl in the sink.

Hold one half of the pomegranate over the bowl, seeds facing down. With the other hand, use a wooden spoon or heavy object to repeatedly whack the back of the pomegranate–hard.

Be careful not to hit your fingers. OUCH!

Seeds will come showering out. Once all of the seeds are out of both halves, pluck out and discard any bitter white parts from the bowl. Store seeds, along with their juices, in a container in the refrigerator for quick access throughout the week.

Use within 7 days.

P.S. You may not want to be wearing white clothes when you do this! If I'm not careful, my kitchen resembles a murder scene.

REFRIGERATOR REORG

What could a li'l refrigerator reorg do for you?

I've seen people reorganize their fridge by following this simple advice, and it has made a world of difference in their households' eating habits.

Before you shop, start with a rather empty fridge. You want to be able to see the back of your fridge. Get up in there.

Toss out those duplicate dressings, consolidate those three jars of salsa, toss the old wilted veggies; we are starting anew–no more waste from here on out. Going forward, you will know exactly what is in that fridge, and you will know that everything is edible and fresh.

Get intimate with your fridge; this is your new restaurant.

Rearrange the height of your fridge shelves. Yes, you can do that. Stop hurting your back, *jeesh.*

Pull everything to the front, so you know what is in there. NOTHING should be shoved to the back; that is where things go to rot. Gross.

Top shelf:

Store all items that must be eaten first. Leftovers, hard-boiled eggs, chopped veg, baked potatoes, dips, chopped veggie sticks, yogurt–you get the point. Let's be honest, we all grab for whatever is on that top shelf. Keep this prepared stuff here at eye level, so you eat it before it goes bad. You will always know what you have and how new it is. When you are hungry, BOOM right there, top shelf, you see all your possibilities. What needs to get eaten first? Grab and assemble.

Bottom Shelf:

Keep your tub of Mixed Salad in an easy-to-grab spot as you will be pulling from it often as the base of many meals.

Raw meat should always be wrapped well and stored in the lowest part of your fridge, so it does not drip onto other food items.

Bins:

Cheeses and tortillas in the cheese bin. Always. You leave that cheese on the top shelf, out in the open, and you know you will straight up eat cheese for dinner.

Fruits and vegetables in the produce bins. You have the recipes; you have a plan for each and every item. DO NOT LET THEM ROT DOWN THERE. Keep them in rotation. You got this.

LABEL IT!

In a restaurant every single item in the refrigerator is labeled with masking tape. It's not being anal; it's called communication. It lets everyone know what needs to be used up first.

Heck, I even label the fridge shelves with masking tape so everyone in the house knows where stuff is–condiments, dressings, international. There is no shame in my game; labels make it easier for everyone. Who has time to search around in the fridge? Note: This simple labeling has also been successful in organizing people's cupboards and pantry.

If you see things starting to get put back in the wrong places, reorganize, and remind your household, "Top shelf is for leftovers!" Run a tight ship at your restaurant. People are trainable. Before you know it, everyone will appreciate knowing exactly where everything lives in the fridge.

Now that's a sexy fridge!

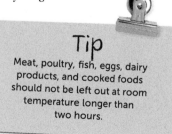

Tip

Meat, poultry, fish, eggs, dairy products, and cooked foods should not be left out at room temperature longer than two hours.

TOMATO JELLY

(16 Servings — uses only ⅓ package)

1 envelope Knox Sparkling Gelatine
¼ cup cold water
2 cups canned or fresh tomatoes
½ bay leaf (if desired)
½ teaspoonful salt
Few grains cayenne or black pepper
1 tablespoonful mild vinegar or
lemon juice
1 tablespoonful mild onion juice
Stalk celery

Mix tomatoes, bay leaf, salt, celery and pepper and boil ten minutes. Pour cold water in bowl and sprinkle gelatine on top of water. Add to hot mixture and stir until dissolved. Add vinegar and onion juice (extracted by grating onion). Strain and turn into molds that have been rinsed in cold water and chill. When firm, unmold on lettuce and garnish with mayonnaise or cooked dressing. Or the jelly may be cut in any desired shape and used as a garnish for salads or cold meats.

NOTE: Tomato soup diluted with an equal quantity of water, or tomato juice, or tomato juice cocktail may be used instead of the canned or fresh tomatoes.

VARIATIONS

1. *Pepper Salad.* Remove core and seeds from large green peppers. When Tomato Jelly begins to stiffen, fill prepared peppers. When firm, slice and serve it to a person, garnishing with lettuce, salad dressing and a slice of hard cooked egg or a cheese ball.

2. *Tomato Shrimp Salad.* When Tomato Jelly begins to stiffen, add 1 cup flaked shrimps and ½ cup finely cut celery. Chicken, tuna fish or crabmeat may be used instead of the shrimps.

3. *Favorite Salad.* When Tomato Jelly begins to stiffen, add ½ cup diced celery and ½ cup chopped almonds or other nuts.

SAVORY PICNIC HAM

Place picnic ham fat side up on rack in shallow pan in slow oven (300°). Allow 32 minutes per pound. Remove rind and score fat. Glaze with 1 cup currant jelly and 1/ cup prepared horseradish, beaten together. Bake in hot oven (400°) until well glazed, basting often with glaze in pan.

Waldorf Salad.

WEIGHTS and MEASURES

CONTENTS of STANDARD CANS

ABBREVIATIONS

OVEN TEMPERATURES

FOR OVEN-CHART SEE INSIDE BACK COVER

Run to your lover!
Let the white heat sear your soul with
purifying passion.
Cry out against the gnawing conflict,
Burn the vision of that other face, and
Listen to your lover.

Hide!

But afterwards
When the cool moon illuminates the bare wall
Where that Irish picture was,
What then?

Yellow Week

AKA CRANK UP THE COLOR

MENU

Theme: American
Prep Day Length: 1½ hours
Total Meals for the Week: 70%

PREP DAY RECIPES
Granola, *p. 78*
Mixed Salad, *p. 79*
Trail Mix, *p. 79*

BREAKFAST
Granola on Yogurt
Quick Omelet aka Quomelet, *p. 102*
Rice Cakes with Almond Butter, Bananas, and Honey, *p. 80*
Fried Eggs with Leftovers, *p. 80*

LUNCH
Rainbow Salad, *p. 82*
Mexican-Inspired Salad, *p. 82*
Leftovers from Dinner:
Salmon on Rainbow Salad
Hearty Vegetarian Chili on Rice
Turkey Burger on Salad

DINNER
Salmon and Mashed Potatoes (*p. 84*), served with
Steamed Summer Squash (*p. 67*)
Hearty Vegetarian Chili on Rice, *p. 86*
Turkey Burgers with Honey Mustard (*p. 88*) served with
Sweet Potato Wedges (*p. 87*)
Potato Pancakes with Mixed Salad, *p. 90*

EXTRAS
Maddie's Apple Crumble, *p. 91*

PANTRY MUST-HAVES

Items and quantities needed for this entire Week. Do you have them?

FLOUR, PREFERABLY WHOLE WHEAT
½ cup

VANILLA EXTRACT
1 tablespoon

BROWN SUGAR
¾ cup

HONEY
½ cup

UNSALTED BUTTER
1 stick
(8 tablespoons)

EXTRA VIRGIN OLIVE OIL, COLD-PRESSED
½ cup

SAFFLOWER OIL
1 cup

BRAGGS LIQUID AMINOS
½ cup

WORCESTERSHIRE SAUCE
½ cup

APPLE CIDER VINEGAR, UNFILTERED
1 tablespoon

CAYENNE PEPPER
CHILI POWDER
CINNAMON, GROUND

CUMIN, GROUND
GINGER, GROUND
OREGANO LEAVES, DRIED

PEPPER
RED PEPPER FLAKES

SALT
TURMERIC

YELLOW SHOPPING LIST

Read your labels! Make sure every item you put in your cart is
Food That Works approved. See page 18.

Fruit

Bananas: 2

*Granny Smith apples: 3

*Apples: 2 (optional)

Lemons: 2

Vegetables

*Salad greens: 1 (5-ounce) tub, like organic spring mix

*Grape tomatoes: 1 pint

Garlic: 1 head

Avocado: 1 (optional)

Carrots: 1 (1-pound) bag

Yellow onions: 2 large

*Green bell pepper: 1 large

*Red bell pepper: 1 large

Zucchini aka Italian squash: 2

Summer squash aka yellow squash: 2

Cauliflower: 1 small head

*Russet potatoes: 4 large

*Sweet potatoes: 2 of equal size

Fresh Herbs

Scallions: 1 bunch

Specialty Cheese Section

Sharp Cheddar cheese: 1 (8-ounce) block

Fish & Poultry

*Salmon fillet, wild-caught: 1-1½ pounds

*Ground turkey, 95% lean: 1 pound

Baked Goods

Burger buns, whole wheat: 1 package

Pasta, Grains, Nuts

Brown rice, preferably Basmati: 1 (2-pound) bag

Old-fashioned oats: 1 (18-ounce) canister

Rice cakes, plain: 1 package (optional)

Almonds, whole, raw: 1 (1-pound) bag

Pumpkin seeds aka pepitas, raw: 1 (10-ounce) package

Sunflower seeds, raw: 1 (10-ounce) package

Dried fruit: 1 (8-ounce) package like papaya, pineapple, or apricots (for Granola)

Raisins: 1 (12-ounce) box

Cans, Jars, Bottles & More

Kidney beans: 2 (15-ounce) cans

Black beans: 1 (15-ounce) can

Beets, sliced: 1 (15-ounce) can

*Tomatoes, whole, peeled: 1 (28-ounce) can, like Muir Glen Organic Plum Tomatoes

Sardines in water or oil: 1 (3- or 6-ounce) can (optional) —just try it!

Capers: 1 small jar (any size)

Dijon mustard: 1 (7.5-ounce) jar

Maple syrup: 1 (8.5-ounce) bottle

Almond Butter or any nut butter: 1 (16-ounce) jar (optional)

*Applesauce, unsweetened: 1 (15- to 24-ounce) jar

Parchment paper: 1 roll

Refrigerated

Cottage cheese, any style: 1 (16-ounce) container

Greek yogurt, plain, full-fat: 1 (32-ounce) container

*Eggs: 1 dozen

Frozen

Corn: 1 (16-ounce) bag

Asterisk (*) suggests to buy organic

YELLOW PREP DAY

NOW YOU HAVE ALL OF YOUR GROCERIES. With a little forethought, you will have colorful, nutritious meals ready to rock in your fridge. This prep list is strategically designed to get you through this process efficiently; do as much as you can. Ready to multitask? Put on some music. Here we go! We are going to bust through this.

Decide what you want to make for dinner tonight. Keep in mind that after the prep work is completed, you may want something quick and easy.

Suggestion: Mexican-Inspired Salad (page 82).

You will need: measuring cups, measuring spoons, large cutting board with a medium bowl next to it for scraps, chef's knife, grater, and containers and plastic bags to store chopped veggies.

Prep List:
1. Bake Granola
2. Chop vegetables
3. Cut lemon
4. Assemble Mixed Salad
5. Shred Cheddar cheese
   Trail Mix (optional)

Preheat oven to Bake 325°F to bake the granola.
Position a rack in the middle of the oven.

1. Bake Granola:

Granola (page 78). Get granola in oven, set timer. While that bakes, move on to chop vegetables.

2. Chop vegetables:

For definitions of chop, mince, zest, etc., see page 20.

Bell peppers:
1 green bell pepper and 1 red bell pepper—remove stems, core, and seeds; discard them in the scrap bowl. Chop the peppers, and store them together in a container in the refrigerator. Use within 5 to 6 days.

Zucchini and summer squash:
1 zucchini and 1 summer squash—remove and discard the stems and ends in the scrap bowl. Chop the zucchini and squash, and store them together in a container in the refrigerator. Use within 5 to 6 days.

1 zucchini and 1 summer squash—remove and discard the stems and ends in the scrap bowl. Slice them into ½-inch rounds. Store them in a plastic bag in the refrigerator. Use within 5 to 6 days.

3. Cut lemon:

1 lemon—cut into 6 wedges. Place in a plastic bag and refrigerate. Use within 5 days.

How is that granola coming?

4. **Assemble Mixed Salad:**

Mixed Salad (page 79).

Almost done, this last one is quick!

5. **Shred Cheddar cheese:**

Shred half the block of cheese on the large holes of a grater (about 1½ cups) for quick access during the week. Store in the refrigerator in a plastic bag with the air removed. Use within 7 days.

Done! Your fridge should look awesome and organized.

Feeling ambitious?

Trail mix can be made with any leftover nuts, seeds, or dried fruit from the Granola recipe or tidbits of ingredients from past weeks. Trail Mix (page 79).

Chop vegetables continued...

Cauliflower:

If a head of cauliflower is washed and broken down, ready in your fridge, and you have recipes for it, you will be more likely to use it. No more waste–here you go.

1 head cauliflower–peel back any green leaves. On a large cutting board, cut the florets off of the core. Cut them into equal sized chunks. Discard the core and leaves in the scrap bowl.

Rinse the florets in a bowl or strainer; shake dry.

Grab 1 large handful of cauliflower, finely chop it (about 1 cup) for Mixed Salad; set aside.

Place the rest of the florets in a plastic bag with a paper towel and refrigerate. Use these later in Mashed Potatoes (page 84). Use within 7 days.

Onion:

1 yellow onion–chop onion and store in a container in the refrigerator. Use within 7 days.

Reuse your scraps!

Reduce the amount of trash and landfill waste you produce by repurposing the vegetable matter in your scrap bowl.

Feed Yourself: Toss your veggie scraps into a bag in the freezer and keep adding to it each week. Once it is full, use it to make a delicious broth.

Feed the Soil: Find a way to compost your veggie scraps and allow them to biodegrade naturally back into the earth.

Granola

Prep Time: 15 minutes · Cook Time: 25 minutes
Makes: 5 cups

Store-bought granola is expensive and is packed with extra sugar and unnecessary calories. Making your own not only saves you money and weight gain, it also gives you the freedom to make granola exactly the way you like it. This granola can be stored for up to twenty days, so make a big batch and you will be set for a while. Toss some in a glass jar and give it to a friend; it makes a thoughtful gift. Have fun with it!

3 cups old-fashioned oats
½ cup raw almonds, whole, chopped or crushed (your preference)
½ cup raw sunflower seeds
½ cup raw pumpkin seeds
⅓ cup real maple syrup
⅓ cup brown sugar
¼ teaspoon salt
¼ cup safflower oil
2 teaspoons vanilla extract
½-1 teaspoon cinnamon (optional)
½ teaspoon ground ginger (optional)
1 cup chopped dried fruit of your choice

Preheat oven to Bake 325°F. Position a rack in the middle of the oven. Line a large baking sheet with parchment paper.

Combine everything, *except the dried fruit,* in a large bowl.

Mix well, pressing against sides of the bowl to break up the brown sugar.

Spread the mixture out evenly onto the prepared baking sheet. Bake for 25 minutes; set timer. Rotate pan once halfway through baking.

Remove the granola from the oven. Allow to cool.

Pour into a sturdy plastic bag, add the dried fruit, and shake to mix!

Remove the air from the bag, and store in the refrigerator, use within 2 to 3 weeks.

Note: Don't be fooled, granola is not a weight-loss food, and you should use portion control when eating it. For breakfast, sprinkle it on top of a big bowl of yogurt and fruit; use it as a garnish rather than a main attraction. One serving is ¼ cup, so roughly one small handful. This is good to note in case you're like me and want to eat the whole tray!

Eating whole tray = terrible bellyache. I tested it.

Tip

Some grocery stores have a bulk bin section. Buying bulk is beneficial because you are not paying for advertising and wasteful packaging. Make sure the bulk bins at your store are well maintained and have a good turnover rate; this is important to prevent purchasing stale or rancid items. Items I tend to buy in bulk: spices, oats, brown rice, quinoa, nuts, seeds, and dried fruit.

Mixed Salad Yellow Week

Total Time: 3 minutes

Assemble this colorful salad on your Prep Day for easy grabbing throughout the week. Don't even think about it; just dump the ingredients directly into the plastic tub that the salad greens came in. *Voilà!* Your fridge is now a salad bar. This Mixed Salad will serve as a dryish base to build upon with toppings and leftovers. To-go meals can be assembled in minutes and then you are out the door!

This Mixed Salad is deliberately composed of dryish vegetables so that it will last for 7 days in the refrigerator because the "dry" ingredients will not cause the lettuce to wilt prematurely. This is why you don't halve the tomatoes now or chop the carrots. Come on, people, this is healthful food on the fly!

Mixed Salad:

- 1 (5-ounce) tub salad greens
- 1 pint grape tomatoes, rinsed and dried
- 1 cup finely chopped raw cauliflower
- 1 cup chopped zucchini and summer squash
- 3 carrots, scrubbed, rinsed, dried, and thinly sliced into rounds

Open the tub of salad greens.

Remove a small handful to make room in the tub, and store in a plastic bag in the refrigerator. (This can be used later on Turkey Burgers, page 88.)

Dump the tomatoes, cauliflower, zucchini, summer squash, and carrots directly into the Mixed Salad container. Toss lightly with your hands.

Keep covered and refrigerated. Use within 7 days.

Throughout the week, top individual servings of Mixed Salad with the toppings of your choice: Leftovers, cottage cheese, salsa, hummus, chopped veggies, fresh herbs, chopped apples, orange segments, grapes, raisins, nuts, seeds, cheese, olives, canned beans, hard-boiled eggs, cooked grains, chicken or fish.

> ## Tip
>
> A good rule of thumb with salads is to always include a drizzle of olive oil and a squeeze of citrus. Fat and acid help the body absorb nutrients better. Many of the nutrients and vitamins in colorful vegetables are fat soluble, meaning they must be eaten with a fat in order to transport their nutrients into your cells. The acids in tomatoes or citrus have been noted to aid in the absorption of vitamin K found in leafy greens.

Trail Mix

Total Time: 3 minutes

Transform leftover ingredients like nuts, seeds, chocolate chips, cereal, dried fruit, shredded coconut, and raisins into a quick trail mix. *Ta-da!* You just saved yourself a lot of money on packaged trail mix and repurposed those leftover tidbits into a hearty snack. Keep bagged-up servings of these on hand in your desk, gym bag, or Purse Kitchen. No more dollars wasted at the vending machine. Well done!

- Almonds
- Pumpkins seeds
- Sunflower seeds
- Walnuts
- Chocolate chips
- Chopped dried fruit
- Raisins
- Granola
- Anything else you can scavenge from your cabinets.

Dump the above ingredients into a plastic bag and shake.

Quantities do not matter; just add handfuls of the ingredients you like, and it will taste good to you.

Place ½-cup portions into plastic bags, so you can grab them on the go! Or store the trail mix in a glass jar.

BREAKFAST

Rice Cakes with Almond Butter, Bananas, and Honey

Total Time: 2 minutes · Serves: 1

Rice cakes are a low-calorie, low-sodium, crunchy snack that is a healthful replacement for bread. If you think you don't like them, smear them with peanut butter and give them another chance. Rice cakes can be topped with a variety of fixin's: peanut butter and apple; the classic peanut butter and jelly; lettuce, tuna, and hot peppers; Nutella (chocolate hazelnut spread) with shredded coconut for a dessert treat; or even a little red sauce, cheese, and chopped veggies for a mini pizza. I typically buy my supermarket's generic brand, plain, unsalted, or multigrain.

I keep these in my desk at work for the 3:00 p.m. snack attack. Almond butter gives you a dose of protein and healthful fats that will keep you full until dinner. But remember, as with any nut butter (almond, peanut, sunflower, or cashew), it is high in calories and fat. Limit yourself to a 2-tablespoon serving. Get your finger outta that jar!

Tip

When buying fruit, it is important to gauge when it will be ripe and when you plan to use it. To know when fruit is ripe, smell it. Ripe cantaloupe will smell like cantaloupe, and ripe bananas will smell like bananas. Quicken the ripening process, by storing them in a closed paper bag; slow down the ripening process, by storing them in the refrigerator. Or if you have fruit that is going bad, don't let them rot; freeze them, and use them in smoothies later.

Here is a light breakfast that can be assembled in two minutes.

2 rice cakes
2 tablespoons nut butter of your choice (almond, peanut, sunflower, or cashew)
1 banana, peeled and sliced
Honey

Spread 1 tablespoon of nut butter on each rice cake. Top with sliced bananas, and drizzle honey over the top.

Fried Eggs with Leftovers

Total Time: 10 minutes · Serves: 1

This recipe is generic: two fried eggs with <insert leftovers here>. Reheat *any* leftovers from dinner in a nonstick frying pan accompanied with two fried eggs and call it breakfast. Believe me, people will be fighting for those leftovers in the morning. DELISH. Below are some examples. Use the same pan to reduce clean up.

1 teaspoon safflower oil, olive oil, or butter
2 eggs
Salt
Pepper
1 pinch dried oregano
Leftovers: Potato Pancakes
**   Mashed Potatoes**
**   Steamed Summer Squash**

Fried Eggs:

Place a large nonstick frying pan over medium-high heat; add the oil, spread it around with a spatula.

Once the oil is hot, crack the eggs into the pan; sprinkle with salt and pepper.

Allow the eggs to cook until whites are cooked through. Flip with spatula and cook for only 20 seconds if you like your yolk runny. Cook an extra 60 seconds if you like your egg yolk cooked through.

Transfer eggs to a plate; sprinkle oregano on top.

Reheat leftovers in the same pan since it is already hot.

Leftovers: Potato Pancakes

Over medium-high heat, reheat the potato pancakes until they are hot in the middle, approximately 2 to 3 minutes on each side. Cover with a lid to cook faster. Transfer to a plate, top with fried eggs.

Leftovers: Mashed Potatoes and Steamed Summer Squash

Over medium-high heat, reheat leftovers until they are hot, approximately 4 minutes. Cover with a lid to cook faster. Transfer to a plate, serve next to fried eggs.

Rainbow Salad

Total Time: 5 minutes · Serves: 1

The more colors on your plate, the more nutrients and vitamins you are getting. You are the artist, be sure your palate, I mean, plate has a rainbow of color at every meal. FYI: serving size for beans, corn, peas, and cottage cheese is ½ cup. Load it on! Just a thought, since you are already tossing together one of these pretty salads in a to-go container, why not assemble a couple of them? You just saved yourself another $20 on lunches out this week. CHA-CHING!

Use the quantities you wish; this is just a guide.

- ½ cup cottage cheese, any style
- ¼ cup chopped red and green bell peppers
- ¼ cup canned black beans, rinsed well and drained (store extra in a container in the refrigerator)
- ½ cup canned sliced beets, rinsed well and drained (store extra in a container in the refrigerator)
- ¼ cup frozen corn, thawed in warm water and drained
- Optional Toppings: sliced scallions, avocado, sardines, capers, hard-boiled eggs, fresh mozzarella, balsamic vinegar, pumpkin or sunflower seeds
- Extra virgin olive oil
- Salt
- Pepper
- 1 handful Mixed Salad
- 1 lemon wedge (⅙ lemon)

Food for Thought:

List the benefits of bringing your own food (BYOF) to work:
- Nutritious, high-quality food
- Increased energy & productivity
- Cost efficient
-

If you are taking this salad to go, start by putting the dressing and wet ingredients at the bottom of the container so that they don't make the rest of the salad soggy.

In a large to-go container, add cottage cheese, peppers, beans, beets, and corn. Pile on optional toppings if you like. Drizzle olive oil over the top; season with salt and pepper. Top with a generous handful of Mixed Salad. Toss in lemon wedge. Cover and refrigerate.

Before eating, squeeze the juice from the lemon wedge over the salad. Replace the cover, and shake vigorously to toss the salad well and combine the flavors.

Tip

Without realizing it, I used to be a salad separatist, meaning that when I made salads, I kept my vegetables and toppings separate and just the top layer got drizzled with dressing. This caused for dry, mediocre salads and I would find myself picking around the veggies and eating only the "good parts." When I worked at Primo Restaurant, I observed how the salads were assembled and what made them so irresistible. All the ingredients for a salad were combined in a bowl, dressing was added, and then the entire salad was thoroughly hand tossed before it was plated. This coated every morsel with dressing and ensured each bite to be equally delicious. There was no need to pick around because EVERY part was covered in goodness. Lesson learned; shake it up! Toss that salad well right before eating—makes a world of difference.

Mexican-Inspired Salad

Total Time: 5 minutes · Serves: 1

Salad greens, black beans, and cottage cheese = BIG PROTEIN! This salad has Mexican flavors and is full of vibrant colors, which means you are getting tons of nutrients and essential vitamins. It is a great afternoon boost to keep your mind on point. If you are not a fan of Mexican flavors, just leave out the cumin and hot sauce to make a delicious garden salad.

Use the quantities you wish; this is just a guide.

½ cup cottage cheese, any style

¼ cup chopped red and green bell peppers

½ cup canned black beans, rinsed well and drained (store extra in a container in the refrigerator)

½ cup frozen corn, thawed in warm water and drained

1 dash ground cumin

1 dash cayenne pepper

Optional Toppings: hot sauce, sliced scallions, avocado, salsa

Extra virgin olive oil

Salt

Pepper

1 handful Mixed Salad

1 lemon wedge (⅙ lemon)

If you are taking this salad to go, start by putting the dressing and wet ingredients at the bottom of the container so that they don't make the rest of the salad soggy.

Tip

Cottage cheese is a nutritious substitute for creamy dressings. If you buy plain cottage cheese, you can always dress it up yourself by adding your own seasoning like Buffalo sauce, blue cheese crumbles, or chopped fresh herbs (try dill or chives!). You could even turn plain cottage cheese into a sweet snack, by topping it with canned or fresh fruit or fruit preserves!

In a large to-go container, add cottage cheese, peppers, beans, corn, cumin, and cayenne. Pile on optional toppings if you like. Drizzle olive oil over the top; season with salt and pepper. Add a generous handful of Mixed Salad. Toss in a lemon wedge. OUT THE DOOR YOU GO! *Andale! Andale!*

Before eating, squeeze the juice from the lemon wedge over the salad. Replace the cover, and shake vigorously to toss the salad well and combine the flavors.

DINNER

Salmon and Mashed Potatoes served with Steamed Summer Squash

Total Time: 45 minutes · Serves: 4

Parchment packet fish is hands down the best way to cook fish. It is healthful, cooks fast, and comes out perfect every time. Best of all, it needs minimal clean up. There is no pan, no spatula, and no fish smell left in your kitchen. The tightly sealed packets allow the fish to cook in its own steam. You can use any type of fish fillet, combined with any soft vegetables, and any herbs you want. I regularly bake off a bunch of these parchment packets, so that during the week I can grab one and quickly add it to a salad or a hot meal. Fresh steamed fish is a low-fat, protein-packed alternative to canned tuna, or deli meats, which are highly processed. Cooked fish should be used in 3 to 4 days.

If you are making the Steamed Summer Squash, I have included the timing of when to prepare them alongside the fish.

Mashed Potatoes:

1 tablespoon salt

2 potatoes, peeled (if not organic) and roughly chopped

2 cups cauliflower florets, roughly chopped

¼ cup plain full-fat Greek yogurt (optional)

3 tablespoons unsalted butter

Salt

Pepper

Salmon Parchment Packets:

1-1½ pounds fresh salmon fillet (any thin fish fillet will do)

Salt

Pepper

1 lemon, thinly sliced into 8 rounds, discard ends

2 tablespoons capers, with juice

Dried rosemary, thyme, or dill weed

You will need 4 pieces parchment paper, each approximately a 12-inch square.

Preheat oven to Bake 350°F. Position a rack in the middle of the oven.

Mashed Potatoes:

Fill a large pot less than halfway with cold water, add the salt. Bring to a boil over high heat, about 5 minutes. Reduce heat to medium. Add the potatoes and cauliflower. Cook for 20 minutes; set timer. Meanwhile, assemble salmon parchment packets.

Salmon Parchment Packets:

On a cutting board, cut the salmon into 4 equal servings. Equal thicknesses will help them cook evenly.

Place one piece, skin side down, in the center of each piece of parchment paper. Season with salt and pepper. Distribute the lemon rounds, capers, and a little caper juice equally among the packets. Season with generous amounts of herbs of your choice.

Fold up each packet like you would a present. Bring the two long ends of the parchment up over the fish, and fold them together a couple times until the fold rests on the fish. Fold each end, crimping to seal. Tuck the ends under the packet. Do the best you can to create a tight seal so the steam cannot escape.

Place the packets on a large baking sheet, set timer depending on thickness of fish: 10 minutes for ½-inch fillets; 15 minutes for 1-inch fillets. Open one packet, cut into the fish to check for doneness. Some people enjoy salmon a little pink in the middle and others like it cooked through–your preference.

Mashed Potatoes continued...

The potatoes and cauliflower are done when they are soft and easily pierced with a fork. Reserve 1 cup of the potato water, as it is full of flavor and nutrients. Mmm…Drain the rest.

Mash the potatoes and cauliflower with a hand masher or puree with a hand immersion blender. Add the yogurt and butter. Mix well. Add small amounts of the reserved potato water to reach desired consistency, discard the rest. Taste. Add salt and pepper to your liking.

Steam the summer squash, page 67.

Serve the mashed potatoes and squash on a plate with the parchment packet, allowing each person to open their own packet!

DINNER

Hearty Vegetarian Chili on Rice

Total Time: 45 minutes · Serves: 6

Chili like this doesn't need an introduction. This chili is so hearty, dark, and thick, you won't even miss the meat. As always, feel free to substitute any canned bean you like.

Rice:

2 cups brown rice (makes 4 cups cooked)

Chili:

1 tablespoon extra virgin olive oil

1 cup chopped yellow onion

6 cloves garlic, finely chopped

1 (24-ounce) can whole plum tomatoes, with juice

¼ cup Worcestershire sauce

¼ cup Braggs Liquid Aminos

LEFTOVERS:

Freeze leftover chili and rice in individual containers so you can grab an easy frozen meal to go. Then you don't have to thaw a huge block if you only want a single portion.

1 cup chopped red and green bell peppers

1 cup chopped zucchini and summer squash

1 teaspoon ground cumin

1 teaspoon chili powder

1 teaspoon dried oregano

½ teaspoon turmeric

¼ teaspoon cayenne pepper

2 (15-ounce) cans kidney beans, rinsed well and drained

Shredded cheese

Plain full-fat Greek yogurt

Sliced scallions

Rice:

Place rice in a medium pot with a lid.

Cover rice with cold water, scrub it well with your hands, and drain. Repeat until water runs clear, about 3 times. Add 4 cups water. Place over high heat, and bring to a boil. Reduce heat to medium-low, cover, and cook rice for 40 minutes; set timer.

Turn off heat, and fluff with a fork. If there is excess water, pour it off. Return the rice to the warm burner and fluff with a fork until the rice dries out a bit. Cover to keep warm until ready to serve.

Chili:

Place a large nonstick frying pan over medium-high heat. Add the olive oil, heat about 2 minutes. Add the chopped onions; sauté for 2 minutes. Add the garlic; sauté for 2 minutes. Stir frequently to prevent burning.

Pour the juice from the tomatoes into the pan and roughly chop tomatoes on a cutting board. Add to pan along with ½ cup water. Stir in Worcestershire sauce, Braggs, peppers, zucchini, summer squash, cumin, chili powder, oregano, turmeric, and cayenne. Cook for 15 minutes. Stir and taste. Add more spices to your liking.

Allow chili to bubble until it reaches your desired thickness, an additional 10 to 15 minutes. The longer it cooks, the more concentrated the sauce will get. Stir frequently to prevent sticking.

Add the beans to the chili; gently stir without crushing them. Reduce heat to medium; cook for 10 minutes.

Scoop a serving of rice into individual bowls, top with chili and sprinkle with cheese. Add a dollop of yogurt, and garnish with scallions.

Sweet Potato Wedges

Prep Time: 15 minutes · Cook Time: 10 minutes
Serves: 2-4

Sweet potatoes are packed with nutrients and have fewer calories than white potatoes. Also, cooking them in the oven is a more healthful option than deep-frying. So when you are having your next French fry craving, don't deny it, go home and bake a big batch of these. Yum! Your body will thank you. You can certainly try this recipe with white potatoes, and as always, I encourage you to experiment with different seasonings.

Traditional Sweet Potato Wedges

2 sweet potatoes, washed and peeled
2 teaspoons safflower oil
¼ teaspoon salt
⅛ teaspoon pepper

Flavor variations to play with:

Spicy Wedges—generous amounts of paprika, cayenne pepper, ground cumin, dried parsley
Herbed Wedges—1 large pinch crushed dried rosemary, dried oregano, red pepper flakes
Maple Wedges—2 tablespoons real maple syrup

Preheat oven to Broil–High. Position the top rack as high as possible so that the sweet potatoes are about 2 inches from the heat source. Line a large baking sheet with parchment paper.

Carefully cut the sweet potatoes into ½-inch wedges. Keep the size consistent so they cook evenly.

Place the wedges on the parchment paper, add oil, salt, and pepper, and additional spices if desired; toss with your hands to coat.

Arrange the wedges on the prepared baking sheet in one flat layer. Do not overcrowd them or they won't get crispy.

Place in the oven on the top rack, set timer for 5 minutes. Keep a close eye on them and broil until they have a nice black char. Flip once halfway through cooking to char the other side; set timer for another 5 to 7 minutes.

Serve alongside Turkey Burgers on page 88.

To cut wedges hold knife at an angle

DINNER

Turkey Burgers with Honey Mustard served with Sweet Potato Wedges

Total Time: 30 minutes · Makes: 6 to 8 burgers

This burger has seriously bold flavors from the Worcestershire sauce, juicy peppers, and onions tucked inside. While cooking, the ingredients caramelize, which makes the burgers blacken up nicely as though they were cooked on the grill. Don't worry, these babies are not burned, that dark color is pure flavor town. Serve with some oven-baked Sweet Potato Wedges and everyone will be singing your praises.

If you are making the Sweet Potato Wedges, I have included the timing of when to prepare them alongside the burgers.

There are three healthful substitutions going on in this meal:
- *Homemade* honey mustard
- Ground turkey in place of ground beef
- Oats in place of bread crumbs

Nice Buns

Honey Mustard:

4 tablespoons Dijon mustard
1 tablespoon apple cider vinegar
3 tablespoons honey
Juice from 1 lemon wedge (⅙ lemon)

Turkey Burgers:

½ cup chopped yellow onion
1½ cups chopped red and green bell peppers
1 pound ground turkey
1 egg
½–¾ cup old-fashioned or instant oats
3 tablespoons Worcestershire sauce
2 tablespoons Braggs Liquid Aminos or 1 tablespoon low-sodium soy sauce
1 teaspoon dried oregano
½ teaspoon salt
½ teaspoon black pepper
1 dash cayenne pepper
1 dash red pepper flakes

2 tablespoons safflower oil, for frying
½ cup shredded cheese
Whole wheat burger buns
Optional Toppings: salad greens, avocado, pickles, chopped onions

Start the Sweet Potato Wedges, page 87.

Get the wedges prepared and ready to go on the baking sheet; set aside. Wait to broil them until burgers are almost done cooking. Charbroiling the sweet potatoes takes only 10 minutes and should be done right before you are ready to eat so they are hot.

Psst... I reccomend Backyard Brine Pickles on your burger!

Honey Mustard:

Combine the mustard, vinegar, honey, and lemon juice in a bowl, and whisk well to combine. Serve as a condiment for the burger and salad.

Topless

Naked
Wait, I got distracted, are we still talking about burgers?

Turkey Burgers:

Take a second to finely chop the chopped peppers and onions into smaller bits; this will help the burgers stay together better.

Combine the turkey, egg, onions, peppers, ½ cup oats, Worcestershire sauce, Braggs, oregano, salt, pepper, cayenne, and red pepper flakes in a large bowl. Gently fold and combine the ingredients with your hands. Be careful not to squeeze it through your fingers or mix it too much or your burgers will be tough.

Form 6 to 8 patties. If mixture is too wet, sprinkle in a little more of the oats (no more than a ¼ cup). Mixture may stick to your hands a bit, but that is okay. When you are forming your patties, try to get a fairly even distribution of veggies and meat. Do your best to mold the meat around the veggies to hold the burger together. Give them one good final pack and squeeze to hold them together.

Place a large frying pan that has a lid over medium-high heat; add the oil. Once the oil is hot, carefully add the burgers.

Burgers should sizzle when they hit the oil.

Fry the burgers until the bottom is blackened and you see that the meat is cooked halfway up the sides of the burgers. That is a good way to gauge when to flip them. Gently flip with a spatula so they do not fall apart. Cook another 5 minutes so both sides are nicely blackened.

Throw those sweet potato wedges in the oven! Don't forget to watch them carefully.

Cut one burger open a bit to check that the center is cooked to a solid texture. The center should not be pink like a beef burger; poultry must be fully cooked. The entire turkey burger should be one solid color, firm, and juicy.

Top with shredded cheese, and cover with a lid to help it melt quickly; cook until cheese is melted, about 1 minute.

Place the burger on the bun, drizzle with honey mustard, and top with your favorite toppings. Serve with sweet potato wedges or a side of Mixed Salad.

LEFTOVERS:

To enjoy this meal again as a quick lunch, in a to-go container, assemble a Mixed Salad, and throw a Turkey Burger on top. They are deee-licious cold! They also freeze well. Tightly wrap them individually in plastic wrap, then tin foil, and freeze. Be sure to label them, these burgers are too precious to forget about in freezer land!

Potato Pancakes with Mixed Salad

DINNER

Total Time: 35 minutes · Serves: 4

As an adult, I was duped into buying the boxed mix of potato pancakes. Until one day, someone showed me how to make potato pancakes the *real* way from scratch. I realized, "HEY! We don't need no stinkin' boxes!" Potato Pancakes consist of five basic ingredients that we almost always have on hand.

I grew up eating potato pancakes. One slathered with applesauce and the other with sour cream. To this day, I enjoy them both ways, but I use Greek yogurt instead of sour cream. Top your pancakes however you like.

You will need a vegetable peeler, grater, and paper towels.

2 large potatoes, washed and peeled

1 large yellow onion

1 egg

3 tablespoons flour

½ teaspoon salt

½ teaspoon pepper

½ cup safflower oil, divided, for frying

Additional Toppings and Sides:

1 cup canned beets, rinsed well and drained

Handfuls of Mixed Salad

1 cup applesauce and/or 1 cup plain full-fat Greek yogurt

2 scallions, light green and white parts, thinly sliced

Salt

Pepper

Shred the potatoes and place in a large bowl.

Slice the top off the onion and peel it, leaving it whole. To prevent the onion from falling apart as you shred, it is best to hold the onion at the root. Start shredding the cut side until you get close to the root and it is too small to hold.

Add the onions, egg, flour, salt, and pepper to the potatoes. Mix well.

Place a large nonstick frying pan over medium-high heat; add half the oil, and heat it about 5 minutes.

Once the oil is hot, add a large dollop, about ¼ cup, of the potato mixture to pan. Flatten with the back of a spoon or spatula to make a thin pancake. Depending on the size of the pan and what size pancakes you are making, you should be able to fry 2 to 3 pancakes at a time.

Fry for a few minutes. Peek under to see the bottom side, once golden brown, flip with a spatula. Adjust heat accordingly.

Line a plate with paper towels.

Once both sides of the pancakes are crispy and golden brown, transfer them to the lined plate to drain and remove excess oil. Repeat until all of the potato mixture is used. Add the rest of the oil to the pan as needed. As you get towards the bottom of the bowl, gently press the potato mixture against the side of the bowl and discard any extra liquid.

Serve the pancakes with a side of beets and a side of Mixed Salad with toppings of your choice. Top the pancakes with a dollop of applesauce or some Greek yogurt, scallions, salt, and pepper. Or try one of each!

These will be a hit for breakfast served with Fried Eggs, see page 80. Mmm...

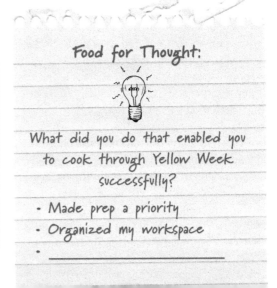

Food for Thought:

What did you do that enabled you to cook through Yellow Week successfully?

- Made prep a priority
- Organized my workspace
- _____

EXTRAS

Maddie's Apple Crumble

Prep Time: 20 minutes · Cook Time: 20 minutes
Serves: 2-3

My dear Australian friend Maddie taught us this easy recipe when we were all living together in the mountains in Turkey at a very special place called Dikencik. Try topping your crumble with some creamy vanilla yogurt. A massive dollop served atop this crumble is a healthful substitute for ice cream. Don't fuss about the size of the dish you bake it in, use whatever you've got.

Apple Mixture:

2 Granny Smith apples, peeled, cut into small chunks
Juice from 3 lemon wedges (½ lemon)
1 teaspoon brown sugar
½ teaspoon cinnamon

Crumble:

½ cup old-fashioned oats
2 tablespoons flour
3 tablespoons brown sugar
1 teaspoon cinnamon
1 dash salt
¼ cup almonds, chopped (any type of nut will do)
4 tablespoons (½ stick) unsalted butter

Vanilla Yogurt:

¾ cup plain full-fat Greek yogurt
1½ teaspoons honey or maple syrup
¼ teaspoon vanilla extract

Preheat oven to Bake 375°F. Position a rack in the middle of the oven.

Apples:

In a medium bowl, combine the apples, lemon juice, brown sugar, and cinnamon. Stir.

Crumble:

In a medium bowl, place the oats, flour, brown sugar, cinnamon, salt, and almonds. Stir.

In a small bowl, heat the butter in the microwave in 10 second increments until melted. Add the butter to the dry ingredients; mix well.

Pour the apple mixture into a small ovenproof baking dish, 8- by 4-inch loaf pan, or an 8-inch pie dish.

Top with the crumble mixture.

Bake for 20 minutes; set timer.

Vanilla Yogurt:

Combine the yogurt, 1 teaspoon water, maple syrup, and vanilla in a small bowl. Stir to mix well.

Remove the apple crumble from the oven; allow to cool for 10 minutes.

Serve warm topped with vanilla yogurt.

A SMALL PORTION
ON PORTIONS

OVEREATING TIRES US out because it creates more work for the body to digest all that food. Besides the obvious issue of weight gain, overeating depletes our natural energy, disrupts our sleep patterns, and affects our hormonal balance. Before I started eating better, I did not realize just how much I was missing out on. Once I started cooking for myself and began eating more whole foods, real foods, I felt fuller longer. Therefore, without much effort, the portions on my plate changed as well. Once my body didn't have to spend so much time working to break down excessive amounts of food,

it had more time to work on other parts of my body, like boosting my immune system, repairing skin cells, reducing wrinkles, making my hair grow faster, and making my nails stronger. I slept better. I felt better. I looked better. All because I was **eating less.** I've realized that when I eat smaller portions, it improves my memory, and increases my energy throughout the entire day. To my surprise, I realized that **the body really does not need that much food at one time!** Whatever motivates you, whether its glowing skin, skinny jeans, or better sleep, smaller portions are the key.

FOOD	TYPICAL SERVING SIZE
DAIRY	
Cottage Cheese	1 cup
Crumbled cheese	¼ cup
Milk	1 cup
Shredded cheese	¼ cup
Yogurt	1 cup
FRUITS	
Apple	1 medium
Banana	½ banana
Blueberries	¾ cup
Mixed Berries	¾ cup
GRAINS, CEREALS, PASTA, RICE	
Cereal	¾-1 cup
Granola	¼ cup
Oats	½-¾ cup
Pasta	½-¾ cup cooked
Rice	½-¾ cup cooked
Rice Cake	2 cakes
PROTEIN	
Beans	½ cup
Eggs	2
Meat and fish	3-5 ounces (size of a deck of cards)
Nut butter	2 tablespoons
Nuts	¼ cup, small handful
Protein powder	1 scoop (see serving size on container)
Seeds	¼ cup, small handful
VEGETABLES	
Baked potato	1 medium
Beets	½ cup
Cooked vegetables (steamed, mashed, broiled, sautéed)	1 cup
Raw vegetables (zucchini, summer squash, onions, bell peppers)	½ cup, 1 large handful
Salad greens (lettuce, spinach)	1-2 cups, two large handfuls
Spaghetti squash	1-2 cups
Sweet potato	1 medium

Listen, I am not a nutritionist and chances are, neither are you. All you need to know is the three components that make a nutritionally balanced meal. **Fat + protein + carbohydrate = superior absorption of nutrients. Do your best to include these three food elements in every meal.** Balanced meals keep you full longer, maximize energy, and increase your body's ability to absorb nutrients. So before you toss that next snack in your mouth—that smoothie, that banana, that bowl of oatmeal—pause, and determine if it has all three components. If not, what can you add to it to make it balanced? For example, don't eat an apple alone (carb); eat it with 10 almonds (fat and protein); now you've got a balanced snack. **Give your body a dose of this trio in every meal and it will seriously thank you.** Think of your body as a machine, a sexy strong machine, I might add. (Wink) Your body is like a car. You cannot run a car without a combination of gasoline, oil, and coolant. If a car ran out of any one of these three, it would not run. So treat your body like the sexy Mustang that it is. *Vroom Vroom*.

Green Week

AKA INTERNATIONAL PALATE

MENU

Theme: Mexican/Southwestern
Prep Day Length: 1½ hours
Total Meals for the Week: 90%

PREP DAY RECIPES
Hard-Boiled Eggs, *p. 35*
Salsa, *p.100*
Instant Oatmeal Packets, *p. 100*

BREAKFAST
Quick Omelet aka Quomelet, *p. 102*
Fresh Apple Cinnamon Oatmeal, *p. 103*
Fresh Banana Nut Oatmeal, *p. 103*
Greek Yogurt Bowl with Fruit, Nuts and Honey, *p. 36*
Smoothies, *p. 124*
Fried Eggs *(p. 80),* or Hard-Boiled Eggs *(p. 35),* with Corn Bread

LUNCH
Curried Chicken Salad, *p. 104*
Taco Salad, *p. 105*
Leftovers from Dinner:
Pulled BBQ Chicken with Corn Bread
Peanut Pad Thai

DINNER
Pulled BBQ Chicken with Corn Bread and Spinach, *p. 106*
Five-Minute Quesadillas with Salsa, *p. 108*
Turkey Tacos with Salsa, *p. 109*
Peanut Pad Thai, *p. 110*

EXTRAS
Trail Mix, *p. 79*
Ants on a Log, *p. 112*
Salsa with Tortilla Chips
Flourless Peanut Butter Cookies, *p. 112*
Blackies (Black Bean Brownies), *p. 114*

PANTRY MUST-HAVES

Items and quantities needed for this entire Week. Do you have them?

FLOUR, PREFERABLY WHOLE WHEAT
1 cup

BAKING POWDER
2 tablesppons

VANILLA EXTRACT
3 teaspoons

BROWN SUGAR
½ cup

SUGAR
2 cups

HONEY
½ cup

EXTRA VIRGIN OLIVE OIL, COLD-PRESSED
½ cup

SAFFLOWER OIL
1 cup

BRAGGS LIQUID AMINOS
½ cup

APPLE CIDER VINEGAR, UNFILTERED
1 teaspoon

CAYENNE PEPPER
CHILI POWDER

CINNAMON, GROUND
CUMIN, GROUND

CURRY POWDER
PEPPER

RED PEPPER FLAKES
SALT

GREEN SHOPPING LIST

Read your labels! Make sure every item you put in your cart is
Food That Works approved. See page 18.

Fruit

Bananas: 5

*Granny Smith apple: 1

*Apples: 2

Lemon: 1

Limes: 2

Vegetables

*Salad greens: 1 (5-ounce) tub, like organic spring mix

*Baby spinach: 1 (5-ounce) bag

*Large-leaf spinach: 1 (8-ounce) bag

Garlic: 1 head

Fresh ginger nub, size of a golf ball

*Celery: 1 (10-ounce) bag

Yellow onions: 2 large

Red onion: 1 small

*Green bell pepper: 1

*Red bell peppers: 2

Green beans: 2 small handfuls (½-pound)

Snow peas: 2 large handfuls (½-pound)

Fresh Herbs

Scallions: 1 bunch

Cilantro: 1 bunch

Specialty Cheese Section

Sharp Cheddar cheese: 1 (10-ounce) block

Poultry

*Chicken breasts, boneless skinless: 1½ pounds

*Ground turkey, 95% lean: 1 pound

Pasta, Grains, Nuts

Pad Thai noodles, soba or udon noodles, or angel hair pasta: 1 package

Cornmeal, stone ground, medium- or coarse-ground: 1 (2-pound) bag

Instant oats aka quick oats, plain: 1 (18-ounce) canister

Almonds, whole, raw: 1 (1-pound) bag

Walnuts, chopped: 1 (6-ounce) bag

Roasted peanuts: 1 (1.75-ounce) small bag, like Planters Cocktail Peanuts

Raisins: 1 (20-ounce) box

Cans, Jars, Bottles & More

Black beans: 1 (15-ounce) can

Refried beans or black beans: 1 (15-ounce) can

*Tomatoes, whole, peeled: 1 (28-ounce) can, like Muir Glen Organic Plum Tomatoes

Chicken broth, low-sodium: 1 (32-ounce) carton, like Imagine Free Range Chicken Broth

BBQ Sauce: 1 bottle (any size)

Hot Sauce: 1 bottle (any size), like Cholula Original or Tabasco

Maple syrup: 1 (8.5-ounce) bottle

Chocolate chips, semi-sweet: 1 (12-ounce) bag

Cocoa powder unsweetened: 1 (8-ounce) canister, like Hershey's Cocoa Powder

Tortilla chips: 1 bag

Peanut butter, smooth: 1 (16-ounce) jar

Vanilla protein powder: 1 container (any size) (optional for Smoothies)

Refrigerated

Greek yogurt, plain, full-fat: 1 (32-ounce) container

*Eggs: 1 dozen

Almond milk unsweetened or milk of your choice: 1 (half gallon) carton

Flour tortillas, whole wheat, large 10-inch: 1 package

Corn tortillas, small 6-inch: 1 package

Frozen

Corn: 1 (16-ounce) bag

*Berries: 1 (15-ounce) bag

Asterisk (*) suggests to buy organic

GREEN PREP DAY

NOW YOU HAVE ALL OF YOUR GROCERIES. With a little forethought, you will have quite the spread of international cuisines to choose from. This prep list is strategically designed to get you through this process efficiently; do as much as you can. Ready to multitask? Put on some music. Here we go! We are going to bust through this.

Decide what you want to make for dinner tonight. Keep in mind that after the prep work is completed, you may want something quick and easy.

Suggestion: Five-Minute Quesadillas (page 108), with Salsa (page 100).

You will need: measuring cups, measuring spoons, large cutting board with a medium bowl next to it for scraps, chef's knife, grater, and containers and plastic bags to store chopped veggies.

Prep List:

1. Bake chicken breasts
2. Hard boil eggs
3. Chop vegetables
4. Make Salsa
5. Shred Cheddar cheese
6. Bag Instant Oatmeal Packets
   Trail Mix (optional)
   Freeze bananas for Smoothies (optional)

Preheat oven to Bake 350°F to bake the chicken breasts.
Position a rack in the middle of the oven. Line a large baking sheet with tin foil.

1. Bake chicken breasts:

Two baked chicken breasts will be for BBQ Pulled Chicken (page 106), and the third will be for Curried Chicken Salad (page 104).

Using one hand, place three chicken breasts on a baking sheet. Using your clean hand, generously salt and pepper both sides of the breasts. Lightly drizzle olive oil on the breasts, and rub it around with your hands to coat them. This creates a barrier to hold in the moisture, preventing chicken from drying out during the baking process. Thoroughly wash your hands and any other items that came in contact with raw chicken.

 Place the chicken in the oven, and bake 25 to 30 minutes, depending on size; set timer.

Once timer goes off, remove chicken and cut into the middle of one breast to check for doneness. The center should be juicy, white, and cooked through, not pink. If it is still pink, cook another 5 to 10 minutes. Allow chicken to cool fully before storing. Store in a container in the refrigerator. Use within 4 days.

2. Hard boil eggs:

Hard-Boiled Eggs (page 35).

3. Chop vegetables:

For definitions of chop, mince, zest, etc., see page 20.

Bell peppers:
1 green bell pepper and 1 red bell pepper–remove stems, core, and seeds; discard them in the scrap bowl. Chop the peppers and store them together in a container in the refrigerator. Use within 5 to 6 days.

Celery:
1 head celery– trim ½ inch off the base and the top of the celery; discard in the scrap bowl. Wash individual celery ribs, removing dirt. Cut ribs into snack-size sticks, about 3 inches long. Store in a plastic bag with a splash of water to keep them moist; refrigerate. Use for Ants on a Log and Curried Chicken Salad. Use within 7 days.

Onions:
2 yellow onions–chop onions and store in a container in the refrigerator. Use within 7 days.

1 red onion–finely chop onion and store in a container in the refrigerator. Use within 7 days.

4. Make Salsa:

Salsa (page 100).

5. Shred Cheddar cheese:

Shred half the block of cheese on the large holes of a grater (about 2 cups) for quick access during the week. Store in the refrigerator in a plastic bag with the air removed. Use within 7 days.

6. Bag 4 Instant Oatmeal Packets:

Instant Oatmeal Packets (page 100).

Done! Your fridge should look awesome and organized.

Feeling ambitious?

Trail mix can be made with any leftover nuts, seeds, or dried fruit from the Granola recipe or tidbits of ingredients from past Weeks. Trail Mix (page 79).

Peel 3 bananas, break them in half, place in large plastic bag, and freeze. Use in Smoothies throughout the week. Mmm…

Reuse your scraps!

Reduce the amount of trash and landfill waste you produce by repurposing the vegetable matter in your scrap bowl.

Feed Yourself: Toss your veggie scraps into a bag in the freezer and keep adding to it each week. Once it is full, use it to make a delicious broth.

Feed the Soil: Find a way to compost your veggie scraps and allow them to biodegrade naturally back into the earth.

PREP DAY RECIPES

lime juice, vinegar, and optional spices. Season with salt. Stir gently to prevent crushing tomatoes. Taste as you go, and add more of any ingredient until it tastes good to you.

Cover with plastic wrap or transfer to a glass jar. Refrigerate, and use within 10 days.

You have just made the freshest salsa money can buy. Remember the flavors will only get better throughout the week as the flavors coalesce.

Use in:
Five-Minute Quesadillas
Turkey Tacos
Taco Salad
Salsa with Tortilla Chips

Salsa

Total Time: 30 minutes · Makes: 2 cups

Once you make fresh salsa, you'll never go back to the stuff in the jar. Serve this Salsa on your Turkey Tacos (page 109), place a scoop atop your Taco Salad (page 105), inside your Quesadilla (page 108), or serve as a snack with chips. In summer, if you have access to flavorful ripe tomatoes, by all means skip the canned! If using fresh tomatoes, simply slice them in half, scoop out the seeds, and roughly chop (you'll need 2 cups). Do not store salsa in a metal bowl as the acidic tomatoes react with metal.

- 1 (28-ounce) can whole peeled tomatoes, rinsed and drained
- ½ cup finely chopped red onions
- 2 cloves garlic, finely chopped
- 4 scallions, light green and white parts, thinly sliced
- ½ bunch fresh cilantro leaves, finely chopped (about 2 tablespoons chopped)
- Juice from 1 lime
- ½-1 teaspoon apple cider vinegar
- 1 dash cayenne pepper (optional)
- 1 dash hot sauce (optional)
- Salt

Roughly chop the tomatoes on a cutting board and place them along with their juices in a glass bowl. Add the onions, garlic, scallions, cilantro,

Instant Oatmeal Packets

Total Time: 5 minutes · Serves: 1

Why make your own instant oatmeal packets? The flavored instant oatmeal packets sold in stores have *eighteen* listed ingredients and loads of sugar. That is not a great way to treat your body first thing in the morning. Prepare the packets yourself and know exactly what is in your oatmeal and save money too. I stash these in my car, Purse Kitchen, gym bag–you name it. In a pinch, I stop at a gas station, fill a small cup halfway with hot water, grab a spoon, add the oatmeal, and bada-bing–clean and nourishing breakfast to go. These are true-life confessions of a gypsy on the road. We have to honor ourselves and make healthful meals a priority. Tricks like this will help you make it happen.

- ½ cup instant oats
- 2 teaspoons brown sugar
- 2 dashes cinnamon
- ¼ cup raisins
- ¼ cup nuts of your choice

Place the oats, brown sugar, cinnamon, raisins, and nuts in a bag; shake until well combined. Done.

When ready to eat:

Place the contents of the oatmeal packet into a mug, add some hot water, stir. Add more water until it reaches your desired consistency.

Tip

You can quickly transform old-fashioned oats into instant oats by chopping them up into smaller bits. This reduces their cook time, thus making them instant oats. Old-fashioned oats can be chopped with a hand immersion blender, food processor, blender, or by mowing over them with a knife.

BREAKFAST

Quick Omelet
aka Quomelet

Total Time: 15 minutes · Serves: 1

Never thought you had enough time to cook an omelet before work? You do when all the veggies are chopped! Omelets are a wonderful way to use up leftovers at the end of the week; almost anything can be tucked into an omelet. Minimal clean up, you dirtied only one pan, one bowl, one spatula, and one fork. The secret to a successful omelet is to use a small, 6- to 8-inch, nonstick frying pan. Sometimes an attempt at an omelet comes out looking more like a scramble. Embrace it and move on. It will taste the same; I promise.

The measurements below are just rough guidelines; you don't even have to measure this stuff, just grab handfuls and GO!

2 teaspoons unsalted butter
2 large handfuls chopped veggies (about 1 cup)
Salt
Pepper
Dried oregano
2 eggs
Small handful cheese of your choice
    (about ¼ cup)

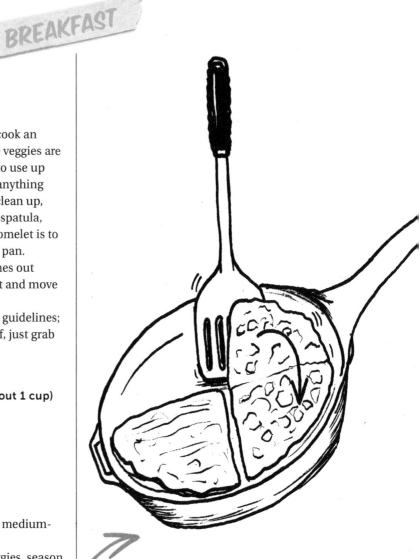

Place a small nonstick frying pan over medium-high heat; add butter.

Once the butter is melted, add the veggies, season with salt and pepper, and stir.

Sauté the veggies about 2 minutes.

While the veggies cook, crack the eggs into a bowl; scramble with a fork.

Add a splash of water (about 2 tablespoons).

Generously season with salt, pepper, and oregano.

Disperse the vegetables around evenly in pan then pour the scrambled eggs over them.

Cook until the eggs are almost completely set up, 4 to 5 minutes.

Sprinkle with cheese.

Use a spatula to loosen the sides of the omelet.

You may need to tip the pan around to bring the uncooked egg to the edges to cook.

Fold one side over the other. Give the omelet a press with the spatula.

Cook until eggs are solid and cheese is melted, about 1 minute. Flip once if necessary.

Garnish with oregano and serve.

Tip

If you are making omelets for two people, I recommend making one large omelet (by doubling this recipe) in a large nonstick frying pan. Once the omelet is done you can cut it in half in the pan. The halves are more manageable to flip and plate and both of you actually get to eat at the same time!

Fresh Banana Nut Oatmeal

Prep Time: 10 minutes · Serves: 1

1 banana, peeled and sliced
1½ teaspoons brown sugar
¼ teaspoon cinnamon
½ cup old-fashioned or instant oats
¼ cup walnuts

Bring 1 cup water to a boil in a medium pot over high heat.

Add the banana, brown sugar, cinnamon, and oats; stir.

Place in a bowl, top with walnuts, and serve.

Tip

Oatmeal never has to be boring; try these delicious additions: peanut butter, cocoa powder, protein powder, fruit preserves, fresh or frozen fruit, chocolate chips, shredded coconut, raisins— just not all together (Wink).

Fresh Apple Cinnamon Oatmeal

Total Time: 10 minutes · Serves: 1

If you have ten minutes before work, this is a great way to start your day. Oats are a cheap and healthful whole grain breakfast option. Be sure to add a fat and a protein to this carb to create a balanced meal that will keep you full longer. You can even make this the night before, refrigerate in a glass jar or a bowl covered with plastic wrap, and simply reheat in the microwave. *Woop woop!*

Below is just a guide; substitute maple syrup or honey if you like. Yep, it is that easy.

1 apple, peeled, cored, and cubed
1½ teaspoons brown sugar
¼ teaspoon cinnamon
½ cup old-fashioned or instant oats
¼ cup nuts

Bring 1 cup water to a boil in a medium pot over high heat. Add the apples, brown sugar, and cinnamon. Reduce the heat to medium, and cook 1 minute; if you prefer your apples soft, cook for 3 minutes.

Add oats; stir until softened, about 2 minutes.

Place in a bowl, top with nuts, and serve.

LUNCH

Curried Chicken Salad

Total Time: 20 minutes · Serves: 2

This chicken salad *rocks*! It is *even better* the next day when all the flavors have fused. That is why I suggest making this in advance, so you have an incredible lunch awaiting you tomorrow. Use plain Greek yogurt as a healthful substitute for mayonnaise. You can serve this chicken salad on a bed of lettuce or rolled up in a whole wheat flour tortilla.

If you absolutely do NOT like the flavor of curry, swap in other dried herbs like dill weed, oregano, rosemary, or tarragon.

- 1 baked chicken breast (from Prep Day page 98), cut in bite-size cubes
- 1 Granny Smith apple, peeled, cored, and finely chopped
- 8 sprigs fresh cilantro, finely chopped
- ¼ cup finely chopped red onions
- ½ cup raisins
- 7 celery sticks, chopped
- ¼ cup plain full-fat Greek yogurt
- 1 tablespoon extra virgin olive oil
- 2 teaspoons Braggs Liquid Aminos
- 2 teaspoons curry powder
- Dash of turmeric (if you have it)
- Salt
- Pepper
- 1 handful salad greens or a large whole wheat flour tortilla

Place the chicken in a large bowl. Add the apples, cilantro, onions, raisins, and celery. Mix well.

Add the yogurt, olive oil, Braggs, and curry powder. Combine gently by tossing with a large spoon. Season with salt and pepper. Taste, and adjust flavors by adding more spices. If it needs more crunch, add more apples or raisins until it tastes good to you. Add more yogurt if you like your chicken salad creamier.

Serve chicken salad on a bed of salad greens or in a wrap.

Taco Salad

Total Time: 15 minutes · Serves: 1

If you have leftover ingredients from taco night, make Taco Salad! Now you get to enjoy that awesome meal twice! Use Greek yogurt as a healthful substitute for sour cream and you can pile it on, guilt free.

½ cup frozen corn, thawed in warm water and drained

Leftover cooked taco meat (page 109)

½ cup chopped red and green bell peppers

¼ cup finely chopped red onions

¼ cup shredded sharp Cheddar cheese

¼ cup Salsa (from Prep Day page 100)

¼ cup plain full-fat Greek yogurt

Extra virgin olive oil

Ground cumin

Salt

Pepper

Optional Toppings: hot sauce; sliced scallions; avocado; canned black beans, rinsed well and drained; handful of tortilla chips (on the side)

1 generous handful salad greens

1 lime wedge (⅙ lime)

If you are taking this salad to go, start by putting the dressing and wet ingredients at the bottom of the container so that they don't make the rest of the salad soggy.

Add the corn, meat, peppers, onions, cheese, salsa, and yogurt to a large to-go container. Add a drizzle of olive oil. Sprinkle cumin, salt, and pepper on top. Pile on optional toppings if you like. Top with the salad greens. Toss in a lime wedge. OUT THE DOOR YOU GO! *Rapido!*

Before eating, squeeze the juice from the lime wedge over the salad. Replace the cover, and shake vigorously to toss the salad well and combine the flavors. Crush the tortilla chips on top.

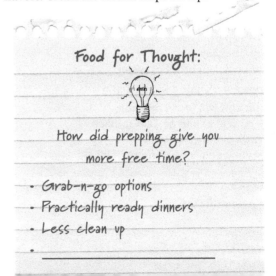

Food for Thought:

How did prepping give you more free time?

- Grab-n-go options
- Practically ready dinners
- Less clean up
-

DINNER

Pulled BBQ Chicken with Corn Bread and Spinach

Total Time: 35 minutes · Serves: 3-4

Pulled BBQ usually refers to a slow process of cooking meat for *hours* until it falls apart into tender succulent shreds. This is my quick rendition so busy working people can still get in their Pulled BBQ fix. The perfect accompaniment to BBQ? Corn bread. There is nothing like the comforting smell of fresh corn bread wafting through your kitchen. And you will have extra for breakfast! Lastly, sautéed spinach completes this colorful plate. Always dress spinach with an acid (like lemon or tomato) and a fat (like olive oil), which allow your body to fully absorb the iron, vitamin K, and other nutrients.

Corn Bread:

½ cup + 1 teaspoon safflower oil to grease pan
¾ cup cornmeal
¾ cup flour
¼ cup + 1 tablespoon sugar
1 teaspoon salt
1 tablespoon baking powder
½ cup unsweetened almond milk or milk of your choice
2 eggs
1 cup frozen corn

BBQ Chicken:

2 baked chicken breasts (from Prep Day page 98)
1 teaspoon extra virgin olive oil
¾ cup chopped yellow onions
3 cloves garlic, finely chopped
1 cup BBQ Sauce
½ cup chicken broth or water

Sautéed Spinach:

¼ cup chicken broth or water
1 (8-ounce) bag large-leaf spinach
Extra virgin olive oil
2 lemon wedges (⅓ lemon)
Salt
Pepper
Red pepper flakes

Preheat oven to Bake 400°F. Position a rack in the middle of the oven.

Grease a muffin tin or an 8- x 8-inch baking dish with the oil, spread with your hands or a paper towel to coat all surfaces.

Corn Bread:

In a large bowl, combine the cornmeal, flour, sugar, salt, and baking powder. Stir together well.

In a medium bowl, combine the remaining ½ cup safflower oil, almond milk, and eggs; "scramble" with a fork. Pour into the dry mixture and stir until batter is combined. Do not overstir; a few clumps are okay.

Add the corn; stir once.

Spoon the batter into the prepared muffin tin, filling each hole three-quarters full. If using a baking dish, simply pour in the batter.

Bake until the tops are firm and golden brown and a knife inserted in the center comes out rather clean, 15 to 20 minutes; set timer.

BBQ Chicken:

While the bread is cooking, place the baked chicken breasts on a cutting board. Hold the meat with one hand and use a fork to scrape the meat towards you in a pulling motion so you get thick stringy pieces of chicken. Or you can pull the chicken breasts apart with your hands. Shred all of the chicken; set aside.

Place a large frying pan over medium heat; add the oil. Once the oil is hot, add the onions; sauté 3 minutes. Add the garlic, and sauté 2 minutes more. Stir in the BBQ sauce and chicken broth. Increase heat to high, and bring to a boil.

Add the shredded chicken, stir to coat, and reduce heat to low. Keep warm, stirring often, until the rest of the meal is ready. Do not overcook the chicken or it can get tough. It is already cooked, you are simply reheating it in the BBQ sauce.

Sautéed Spinach:

Place a large nonstick frying pan over medium-high heat; add the chicken broth. Once steam rises off the broth, add the entire bag of spinach, tearing the leaves as you go–remove massive stems but don't fuss too much, it will cook down.

Cover and steam for 3 to 4 minutes, stir once so spinach cooks evenly. Don't overcook the spinach; you simply want it to wilt. Drizzle olive oil on top, and squeeze lemon juice over all. Sprinkle with salt, pepper, and red pepper flakes.

DING! DING! DING! *Come and get it!*

LEFTOVERS:

Pack leftovers for lunch tomorrow. Or reheat the spinach and corn bread together in a pan with fried eggs for breakfast! For instructions on Fried Eggs, see page 80.

Five-Minute Quesadillas with Salsa

Total Time: 5 minutes · Serves: 2

In a serious rush? No worries, you can still eat healthfully tonight. Since your veggies are already chopped, you can slam this quesadilla together in five minutes flat. No need to measure. I put quantities below only as a guide so you don't skimp on the veggies. A tortilla with melted cheese is not a sufficient meal! Heat up some refried beans or black beans, in a small pot, and BOOM, dinner is ready. Protein in the beans will keep you full, and you'll only have four dishes to clean. *Uh-huh, get your quesadilla on.*

Beans:

1 (15-ounce) can refried beans or black beans, rinsed well and drained
1 small handful chopped yellow onion (¼ cup)
Generous dashes of ground cumin
Generous dashes of hot sauce

Quesadilla:

1 teaspoon safflower oil or extra virgin olive oil
2 large whole wheat flour tortillas
2 handfuls (1 cup) shredded sharp Cheddar cheese
1 dash ground cumin (optional)
1 dash hot sauce (optional)
2 handfuls (1 cup) chopped red and green bell peppers
1 handful (½ cup) chopped yellow onion
Any of your favorite veggies (optional)

For Dipping:

½ cup plain full-fat Greek yogurt
½ cup Salsa (from Prep Day page 100)
Hot sauce

Beans:

Place the beans in a small pot over medium-high heat. Enhance the beans by adding the onions, cumin, and hot sauce. Stir, cook until hot, about 5 minutes.

Quesadillas:

Pour the oil into a large nonstick frying pan over medium-high heat. When the oil is hot, place one tortilla in the pan, and sprinkle a small handful of cheese all over the tortilla. Add the cumin and hot sauce, if using.

Top the tortilla with the peppers and onions, and any of your favorite veggies.

Add the beans onto the tortilla if you like, or serve them as a side.

Fold the tortilla in half, press with a spatula, and cook about 3 minutes. Flip and cook until cheese is melted and quesadilla is golden brown, about 3 minutes more.

Repeat with second quesadilla.

Serve with yogurt, salsa, and hot sauce for dipping, and a side of beans garnished with a little chopped onion or cheese.

If you don't even have five minutes to spare—I've been there—this entire meal can be cooked in the microwave. So technically you can make this at work if you bring the ingredients. But don't tell anyone I told you to do this. Okay?

Microwave Quesadilla—
Place one tortilla on a plate.
Top with cheese and generous handfuls of chopped veggies.
Sprinkle with cumin and hot sauce.
Fold in half, press with hand, and microwave 30 to 40 seconds.
Microwave the refried beans in a separate bowl.

FYI—this quesadilla will be a little soggy since you cheated and microwaved it!

Turkey Tacos with Salsa

Total Time: 35 minutes · Serves: 4

Everyone loves taco night! Here are some easy modifications that make this dish more healthful without sacrificing flavor:

- Change up the protein, and use ground turkey or beans instead of beef.
- Choose beans, for the quickest and cheapest option to get those tacos on the table.
- Use your own spices instead of taco seasoning packets, which are full of chemicals, sodium, and anticaking agents. Yuck.
- Use Greek yogurt instead of sour cream. Get fancy with it! Flavor your Greek yogurt with the same spices you use in the meat, a little lime juice, or just hot sauce! *No hay reglas!*

If you didn't make Salsa on your Prep Day, it takes 15 minutes to make it now, see page 100.

Taco Toppings:

1 cup chopped red and green bell peppers
¼ cup chopped red onions
1½ cups shredded sharp Cheddar cheese
1 cup Salsa (from Prep Day page 100)
½ cup plain full-fat Greek yogurt
2 cups salad greens, chopped

Taco Meat:

2 teaspoons extra virgin olive oil
1 pound ground turkey or 2 cans black beans, rinsed well and drained
1 cup chopped yellow onions
2 teaspoons Braggs Liquid Aminos or ½ teaspoon salt
½ cup chicken broth or water
½ teaspoon ground cumin
¼ teaspoon cayenne pepper
¼ teaspoon red pepper flakes
½ teaspoon chili powder (if you have it)
3 tablespoons Salsa (from Prep Day page 100)
6 sprigs fresh cilantro, roughly chopped
Juice from 2-3 lime wedges (⅓ to ½ lime)
Tabasco (optional)
1 package small corn tortillas

LEFTOVERS:
Prepare Taco Salads for tomorrow's lunch, see page 105.

Taco Toppings:

Most of these items are already chopped and in your fridge. Arrange the peppers, red onions, cheese, salsa, yogurt, and greens in small bowls with serving spoons.

Preheat oven to Bake 350°F. Position a rack in the middle of the oven.

Taco Meat:

Place a large nonstick frying pan over medium-high heat; add the oil. Add the turkey; break it up with a spatula into chunks. As it cooks, continue to break it up in to smaller chunks, and stir to ensure all sides cook through, about 5 minutes.

Once the meat is browned, add the onions.

Then add the Braggs, broth, cumin, cayenne, red pepper flakes, chili powder, and salsa; mix well. Cook 2 minutes, stirring frequently as it starts to thicken. Reduce the heat to low to keep warm.

Add the cilantro, lime juice, and several dashes Tabasco. Stir, taste, and adjust by adding more seasonings until it tastes good to you.

Carefully hang the tortillas directly on your oven racks, see illustration above. Or spread the tortillas out on a large baking sheet. Heat 10 to 15 minutes; set timer.

Transfer the tortillas to a plate, and cover with tin foil to keep warm. Everything is ready for your taco fiesta!

Peanut Pad Thai

Total Time: 40 minutes · Serves: 4-6

This Thai-inspired dish is made with stir-fried rice noodles. When I cannot find rice noodles at the store, I substitute another noodle like soba, udon, or angel hair pasta. Alternatively, I serve it on a bed of rice, which technically makes this dish a Peanut Stir-Fry. If using rice, start the rice first as it takes the longest. For directions on cooking rice, see the Hearty Vegetarian Chili recipe on page 86. No matter what you serve it on, the combined flavors of ginger, peanut, and soy sauce will have people coming back for more.

Vegetables:

2 small handfuls fresh green beans, washed, tops and tails removed

2 large handfuls fresh snow peas, washed

1 red bell pepper, remove stem and core with seeds, and cut into ½-inch strips

Peanut Sauce:

¼ cup Braggs Liquid Aminos or low-sodium soy sauce

1-1½ cups chicken broth

¼ cup smooth peanut butter

1 teaspoon red pepper flakes

¼ cup sugar

1 fresh ginger nub, size of a golf ball

8 scallions, light green and white parts, thinly sliced

Assembly:

1 package Asian noodles

¼ cup unsalted roasted peanuts, crushed

4 sprigs fresh cilantro, chopped

Vegetables:

Heat ¼ cup water in a large nonstick frying pan over medium heat. Once steam rises off the water, add the green beans, snow peas, and red peppers. Cover and steam for 5 minutes only; set timer. Remove the lid, and set the pan aside. Do not overcook the vegetables as they will get cooked more later.

Peanut Sauce:

In a medium mixing bowl, place the Braggs, chicken broth, peanut butter, red pepper flakes, and sugar; whisk well to combine.

On a cutting board, finely grate the entire ginger nub, skin and all. Place grated ginger in your palm and squeeze the juice directly into the mixing bowl. Discard the pulp after squeezing. Add most of the scallions, save some for garnish.

Assembly:

Boil noodles according to package directions. Drain well.

Pour the Peanut Sauce into the pan of steamed vegetables. Place the pan over high heat and cook until the sauce bubbles and starts to thicken, about 4 minutes. Stir.

Add the noodles. Toss gently to coat. Taste sauce and adjust seasonings to your liking.

Plate the Pad Thai, and garnish with peanuts, cilantro, and remaining scallions.

Tip

Warming foods, like ginger, scallions, cayenne, and garlic, have higher thermal levels, meaning they influence the heat that the human body puts off. It is important to incorporate warming foods into your diet during the colder months to warm the body, boost the immune system and help fight colds. Ever wonder why you start sweating when you eat a garlicky dish? *Wooo-wheee!* On the other hand, cooling foods, like melon, cucumber, and peppermint, have cooling properties to help you cope with the heat in the summer months.

LEFTOVERS:

This dish is delicious cold as well; take leftovers for lunch. Next time, try adding your favorite protein, like cooked chicken, shrimp, or tofu. At the end of cooking, simply add the protein and toss to coat.

EXTRAS

Ants on a Log

Total Time: 5 minutes · Serves: 1

Here is a quick snack to use up that celery and peanut butter. Okay, so it's really just a vehicle to get the peanut butter into my mouth. The hardest part is remembering that a serving of nut butter is two tablespoons. *Ugh. Put the jar down, Malia. Put it down.*

2-3 celery sticks
2 tablespoons peanut butter
2 tablespoons raisins

Spread the peanut butter on the celery sticks. Sprinkle raisins on top. Eat.

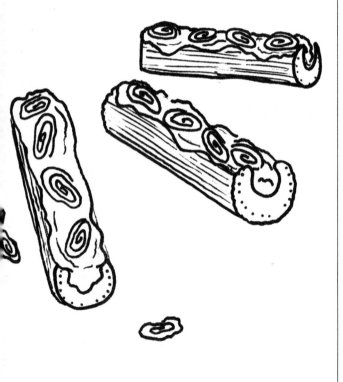

Flourless Peanut Butter Cookies

Prep Time: 20 minutes · Cook Time: 15 minutes
Makes: 24 cookies

Want a cookie? Sometimes you need a cookie. That is natural, but cookies out of a package *are not*. Read the listed ingredients on the cookie package. Over *forty-two* listed ingredients? That should be reason enough to not eat them. Cookies are basic and require anywhere from six to twelve ingredients. You can eat cookies anytime; you just have to *make them yourself*. Besides, nothing beats a warm cookie right out of the oven, right? This recipe is so fast to make, don't even bother getting out the flour. Without flour in the way, you get straight down to that peanut butter flavor. As always, get creative with it.

1 egg
1 cup sugar
1 cup smooth peanut butter
1 teaspoon vanilla extract
½ teaspoon baking powder
Salt
Optional Toppings: chocolate chips or jam

Preheat oven to Bake 350°F. Position a rack in the middle of the oven. Line a large baking sheet with parchment paper for easy clean up.

Crack the egg into a medium bowl; lightly scramble with a fork. Add the sugar, peanut butter, vanilla, and baking powder. Mix well.

Roll the dough between your palms into balls a little smaller than golf balls. Place on the prepared baking sheet about 1 inch apart.

Use a fork to flatten the balls and create a crisscross pattern. If adding toppings to your cookies, instead of flattening the balls, press your thumb into the center of each ball, creating a hole to fill with chocolate chips or jam.

Sprinkle the cookies with a little salt.

Place in the oven on the middle rack. Bake until golden around the edges, about 15 minutes. Set timer.

Slide the parchment paper off the baking sheet and onto a cool surface like a counter top. Let cookies cool completely.

Blackies (Black Bean Brownies)

EXTRAS

Prep Time: 25 minutes · Cook Time: 35 minutes
Chill Time: refrigerate overnight · Serves: 10

You trusted me enough to buy this book. Now you just need to trust me on this one. To everyone's amazement, these Blackies are fudgy and delicious. You won't taste one single bean. No one *ever* needs to know these brownies have beans in them. Blackies are packed with protein and have half the carbs and sugar of traditional flour brownies. I know what you are thinking—just rinse the beans really well to remove the starches and sugars that disrupt the stomach. The hardest part is resisting eating these immediately after they come out of the oven, but they actually taste better after a night in the fridge.

I added this variation for more healthful brownies to show that *anything* can be modified to be more healthful. *Anything*. Even brownies. Go ahead, give it a try. You won't be mad at me.

You will need a hand immersion blender, food processor, or blender.

- **2 teaspoons safflower oil to grease pan**
- **1 (15-ounce) can black beans, rinsed well and drained**
- **½ cup instant oats**
- **¼ cup cocoa powder, unsweetened**
- **½ teaspoon baking powder**
- **¼ teaspoon salt**
- **¼ cup safflower oil**
- **2 teaspoons vanilla extract**
- **¼ cup honey**
- **¼ cup maple syrup or packed brown sugar**
- **½ cup semisweet chocolate chips**
- **½ cup chopped walnuts**

Preheat oven to Bake 350°F. Position a rack in the middle of the oven.

Grease an 11- by 7-inch baking pan or 8-inch square baking pan (glass, ceramic, or tin) with oil, spread with your hands or a paper towel to coat all surfaces.

Place the beans in a deep mixing bowl. Add the oats, cocoa powder, baking powder, salt, oil, vanilla, honey, and maple syrup; mix well.

Puree using a hand immersion blender, food processor, or blender until completely smooth.

Add the chocolate chips, stir. Taste. YUM.

Pour batter into baking dish; smooth out top with back of a spoon.

Sprinkle with the walnuts, gently pat them down into the batter so they stay on the brownies.

Bake on the middle rack until the center of the brownies are firm. Set timer for 35 minutes.

Allow to cool fully. Cover with plastic wrap, and refrigerate overnight.

Cut the brownies and serve cold.

Tip: Next time, get adult fancy and add a splash (1 tablespoon) of dark rum, bourbon, kirsch cherry liquor, a handful of shredded coconut, or a sprinkle of cayenne pepper to your batter. Oh my!

Endicott Rock Bathing Beach, The Weirs, Lake Winnipesaukee, N.H.

Mr. George Wm. Putnam
443 Orange Road
Montclair
New Jersey

Barten Baadesstr. 49, D-8000 Mün

700.00 DEPOSIT

not long
Nancy,
not long
good Gr
not long

Orange Week

AKA AMBITIOUS ONE

MENU

Theme: Mexican/Italian
Prep Day Length: 2 hours
Total Meals for the Week: 90%

PREP DAY RECIPES
Mixed Salad, *p. 122*
Quick Salsa, *p. 122*

BREAKFAST
Beastly Breakfast Bowl with Spaghetti Squash, *p. 123*
Smoothies, *p. 124*
Malia's Enlightened "Eggs Benedict", *p. 126*
Greek Yogurt Bowl with Fruit, Nuts, and Honey, *p. 36*
Quick Omelet aka Quomelet, *p. 102*

LUNCH
Pasta Salad, *p. 128*
Leftovers from Dinner:
Baked Mac and Cheese
Turkey Meatballs or Meatball sub
Black Bean Enchilada

DINNER
Tuna Melt, *p. 129*
Sweet Potato Quesadillas *(p. 130)*, with Quick Salsa *(p. 122)*
Southwestern Baked Mac and Cheese, *p. 132*
Turkey Meatballs with Robust Tomato Sauce over Spaghetti Squash, *p. 134*
Black Bean Spinach Enchilada Bake, *p. 136*

EXTRAS
Baked Sweet Potatoes, *p. 137*
Apples, veggie sticks, or rice cakes with sunflower butter
Garlic Bread (optional), *p. 137*
Morning Glory Muffins, *p. 138*

PANTRY MUST-HAVES

Items and quantities needed for this entire Week. Do you have them?

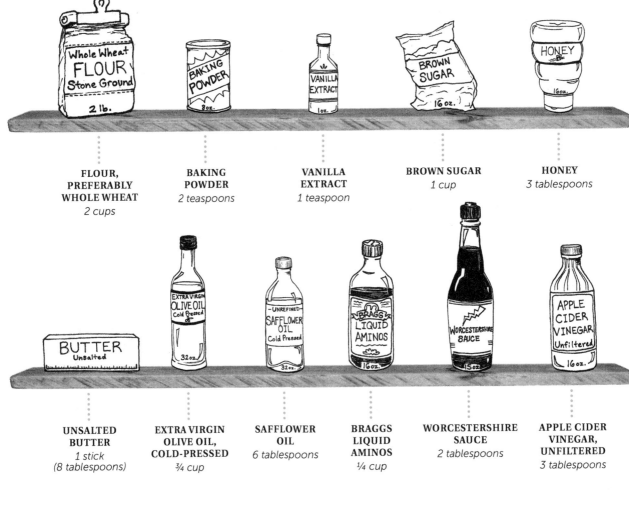

FLOUR,
PREFERABLY
WHOLE WHEAT
2 cups

BAKING
POWDER
2 teaspoons

VANILLA
EXTRACT
1 teaspoon

BROWN SUGAR
1 cup

HONEY
3 tablespoons

UNSALTED
BUTTER
1 stick
(8 tablespoons)

EXTRA VIRGIN
OLIVE OIL,
COLD-PRESSED
¾ cup

SAFFLOWER
OIL
6 tablespoons

BRAGGS
LIQUID
AMINOS
¼ cup

WORCESTERSHIRE
SAUCE
2 tablespoons

APPLE CIDER
VINEGAR,
UNFILTERED
3 tablespoons

BASIL LEAVES, DRIED
BAY LEAVES (OPTIONAL)
CAYENNE PEPPER
CHILI POWDER

CINNAMON, GROUND
CUMIN, GROUND
FENNEL SEEDS
GINGER, GROUND

OREGANO LEAVES, DRIED
RED PEPPER FLAKES
SAGE, GROUND

THYME LEAVES, DRIED
PEPPER
SALT

ORANGE SHOPPING LIST

Read your labels! Make sure every item you put in your cart is
Food That Works approved. See page 18.

Fruit

Bananas: 5

Lemon: 1

Limes: 2

*Apple: 1 (optional)

Vegetables

*Baby spinach: 1 (5-ounce) tub

*Large-leaf spinach: 2 (8-ounce) bags

*Grape tomatoes: 1 pint

Garlic: 1 head

Carrots: 1 (1-pound) bag

*Celery: 1 (10-ounce) bag

Yellow onions: 3

Red onion: 1 small

*Green bell peppers: 3

*Red bell pepper: 1

Asparagus: 1 bunch

Zucchini aka Italian squash: 3

Summer squash aka yellow squash: 3

Spaghetti squash: 1 small

*Sweet potatoes: 3 of equal size

Fresh Herbs

Scallions: 1 bunch

Cilantro: 1 bunch

Specialty Cheese Section

Sharp Cheddar cheese: 1 (16-ounce) block

Meat & Poultry

Prosciutto: 1 package, 4-6 slices, or ¼-pound

*Ground turkey, 95% lean: 1 pound

Baked Goods

French baguette: 1 (buy fresh the day you are making Malia's En*lightened* "Eggs Benedict")

Pasta, Grains, Nuts

Pasta, whole wheat, spirals or macaroni: 1 (16-ounce) bag/box

Instant oats aka quick oats, plain: 1 (18-ounce) canister

Rice cakes, plain: 1 package (optional)

Sunflower seeds, raw: 1 (10-ounce) package

Raisins: 1 (12-ounce) box

Cans, Jars, Bottles & More

Black beans: 1 (15-ounce) can

Corn: 1 (15-ounce) can

Green chiles, diced or chopped: 2 (4-ounce) cans

*Tomatoes, whole, peeled: 1 (28-ounce) can, like Muir Glen Organic Plum Tomatoes

*Tomatoes, diced: 1 (15-ounce) can, like Muir Glen Organic Diced Tomatoes

*Tuna in water: 2 (5-ounce) cans, like Wild Planet

Buffalo sauce: 1 bottle (any size), like Frank's RedHot Buffalo Wing

Capers: 1 small jar

Sunflower butter or any nut butter: 1 (16-ounce) jar (optional)

Red wine: 1 bottle, like merlot or cabernet sauvignon (optional for cooking & drinking!)

Vanilla protein powder: 1 container (any size) (optional for Smoothies)

Refrigerated

Cottage cheese, country style small curd, plain: 1 (16-ounce) container

Cottage cheese, any style: 1 (16-ounce) container, like Hood Cottage Cheese and Chive

Greek yogurt, plain, full-fat: 1 (32-ounce) container

*Eggs: 1 dozen

Almond milk, unsweetened, or milk of your choice: 1 (half gallon) carton

Flour tortillas, whole wheat, large 10-inch: 1 package

Corn tortillas, small 6-inch: 1 package of 8

Frozen

*Berries: 1 (15-ounce) bag

Asterisk (*) suggests to buy organic

ORANGE PREP DAY

NOW YOU HAVE ALL OF YOUR GROCERIES. With a little forethought, you will have delectable dishes for days. This prep list is strategically designed to get you through this process efficiently; do as much as you can. Ready to multitask? Put on some music. Here we go! We are going to bust through this.

Decide what you want to make for dinner tonight. Keep in mind that after the prep work is completed, you may want something quick and easy.

Suggestion: Southwestern Baked Mac and Cheese (page 132).

You will need: measuring cups, measuring spoons, large cutting board with a medium bowl next to it for scraps, chef's knife, grater, and containers and plastic bags to store chopped veggies.

Prep List:
1. Bake spaghetti squash
2. Bake sweet potatoes
3. Cut lemon
4. Chop vegetables
5. Assemble Mixed Salad
6. Make Quick Salsa
7. Shred Cheddar cheese
   Bag Instant Oatmeal Packets (optional)

Preheat oven to Bake 400°F to bake the spaghetti squash and sweet potatoes. Position a rack in the middle of the oven.

1. Bake spaghetti squash:

1 spaghetti squash–carefully cut in half lengthwise through the stem end. Scrape out seeds with a spoon; discard the seeds in the scrap bowl.

Place the two halves (cut-side up) in a baking dish; add 2 cups water into the bottom of the dish. Place on the rack in the oven, all the way over to one side. Lay a sheet of tin foil directly on the oven rack next to the spaghetti squash for the sweet potatoes so they don't drip everywhere.

2. Bake sweet potatoes:

2 sweet potatoes–scrub well, dry with a towel. Gently stab each potato several times with a fork to prevent exploding–you know how I feel about cleaning. Use your hands to rub the potatoes with a little olive oil. This makes the skins easy to peel. Place the sweet potatoes on the tin foil. Bake 1 hour, set timer.

Spaghetti squash and sweet potatoes will be done at roughly the same time.

3. Cut lemon:

1 lemon–cut into 6 wedges. Place in a plastic bag and refrigerate. Use within 5 days.

4. Chop vegetables:

For definitions of chop, mince, zest, etc., see page 20.

Zucchini:
2 zucchini–remove and discard the stems and ends into the scrap bowl. Chop the zucchini and store in a container in the refrigerator. Save other zucchini for Morning Glory Muffins. Use within 5 to 6 days.

Summer squash:
3 summer squash–remove and discard the stems and ends into the scrap bowl. Chop the squash and store in a container in the refrigerator. Use within 5 to 6 days.

Asparagus:
1 bunch asparagus–trim the tough woody ends (about 1 inch) off the base of the asparagus; discard in the scrap bowl. Chop the asparagus into 1-inch pieces, place in a container in the refrigerator. Use within 4 to 5 days.

Bell peppers:
3 green bell peppers– remove stems, core, and seeds; discard them in the scrap bowl. Chop the peppers and store in a container in the refrigerator. Use within 5 to 6 days.

1 red bell pepper–remove stems and core with seeds; discard them in the scrap bowl. Chop the peppers and store in a container in the refrigerator. Use within 5 to 6 days.

Celery:
4 ribs celery–trim ½ inch off the base and the top of the celery; discard in the scrap bowl. Wash individual ribs, removing dirt. For quicker chopping, cut celery into long strips, stack them on top of each other, and then finely chop celery by cutting across the strips (about 2 cups). Store in a plastic bag with a splash of water so they don't dry out; refrigerate. Use within 7 days.

Carrots:
2 large carrots–scrub, rinse, dry, and slice carrots into thin rounds for Mixed Salad; set aside. Use within 7 days.

Optional:
Cut up the rest of the carrots and celery into sticks for easy snacks on the go. Bag serving-size portions, add a splash of water to the plastic bags to keep them moist, and refrigerate. For a snack, try dipping them in sunflower butter!

Chop vegetables continued...

Onions:
3 yellow onions–chop onions and store in a container in the refrigerator. Use within 7 days.

1 red onion–finely chop onion and store in a container in the refrigerator. Use within 7 days.

Almost done, these last ones are quick!

5. Assemble Mixed Salad:
Mixed Salad (page 122).

6. Make Quick Salsa:
Quick Salsa (page 122).

7. Shred Cheddar Cheese:
Shred the whole block of cheese for quick access during the week. Store in the refrigerator in a plastic bag with the air removed. Use within 7 days.

Done! This was the longest Prep Day. If you tackled all of this work in one day, you are a TROOPER! You should be really proud of yourself right now. I am proud of you.

Feeling ambitious?
Bag Instant Oatmeal Packets to take to work.
Instant Oatmeal Packets (page 100).

How are the sweet potatoes and spaghetti squash doing?

Once timer goes off, sweet potatoes should be easily pierced in the middle with a fork, and the spaghetti squash should be easy to scrape into stringy shreds with a fork. If not, cook them an additional 15 minutes.

Once done, allow the sweet potatoes to cool fully before storing. Wrap in tin foil or in a plastic bag, and refrigerate. Use within 3 to 4 days.

Allow the squash to cool fully before storing. Place the two halves together in a plastic bag, and refrigerate. You can quickly scrape out portions as needed throughout the week. Use within 6 days.

Reuse your scraps!
Reduce the amount of trash and landfill waste you produce by repurposing the vegetable matter in your scrap bowl.

Feed Yourself: Toss your veggie scraps into a bag in the freezer and keep adding to it each week. Once it is full, use it to make a delicious broth.

Feed the Soil: Find a way to compost your veggie scraps and allow them to biodegrade naturally back into the earth.

Mixed Salad Orange Week

Total Time: 3 minutes

Assemble this colorful salad on your Prep Day for easy grabbing throughout the week. Don't even think about it; just dump the ingredients directly into the plastic tub that the baby spinach came in. *Voilà!* Your fridge is now a salad bar. This Mixed Salad will serve as a dry base to build upon with toppings and leftovers. To-go meals can be assembled in minutes, and then you are out the door!

This Mixed Salad is deliberately composed of dryish vegetables so that it will last for seven days in the refrigerator because the "dry" ingredients will not cause the spinach to wilt prematurely. This is why you don't halve the tomatoes now or add shredded carrots.

Mixed Salad:

1 (5-ounce) tub baby spinach
½ pint grape tomatoes, rinsed and dried
1 cup sliced carrots
½ cup raw sunflower seeds

Open the tub of baby spinach.

Dump the tomatoes, carrots, and sunflower seeds directly into the mixed salad container. Toss lightly with your hands.

Keep covered and refrigerated. Use within 7 days.

Throughout the week, top individual servings of Mixed Salad with the toppings of your choice: Leftovers, cottage cheese, salsa, hummus, chopped veggies, fresh herbs, chopped apples, orange segments, grapes, raisins, nuts, seeds, cheese, olives, canned beans, hard-boiled eggs, cooked grains, chicken or fish.

Tip

I know this seems to go against your salad-building instincts, but if you despise a soggy salad, retrain your brain to place the wet toppings like dressing, olive oil, and cottage cheese in your to-go container *first*. Then add a handful of Mixed Salad on top keeping your greens crisp. When you are ready to eat, shake the container vigorously to toss the salad. Ah-ha! Now you might be more apt to prepare your salads for lunch the night before, sans sog!

Quick Salsa

Total Time: 10 minutes · Makes: 1½ cups

This is a speedy recipe for salsa. Really you are just combining the ingredients in a bowl. If you have the time, add the fresh chopped garlic. Why? Because it's good for you!

1 (15-ounce) can diced tomatoes, with juice
¼ cup finely chopped red onions
¼ cup chopped green bell peppers
3 scallions, light green and white parts, thinly sliced
6 sprigs cilantro, finely chopped
½ teaspoon apple cider vinegar
Juice from 3 lime wedges (½ lime)
Salt
2 cloves garlic, chopped (optional)
Hot sauce (optional)
1 dash cayenne pepper (optional)

Place the diced tomatoes with the juice in a glass bowl. Add the onions, peppers, scallions, cilantro, vinegar, lime juice, and salt to taste. Stir. Taste and add optional ingredients or more of any ingredient until it tastes good to you.

Cover and refrigerate to allow flavors to coalesce.

Use in:

Sweet Potato Quesadilla
Black Bean Spinach Enchilada Bake

Beastly Breakfast Bowl with Spaghetti Squash

Total Time: 5 minutes · Serves: 1

This no-brainer breakfast is easy to throw together, even when you're still half asleep. A serving size of oats is a measly ½ cup. A big bowl of oatmeal can quickly add up to over 550 calories after you add nuts, fruit, and sweetener. Instead, use spaghetti squash as a delicious filler. This beastly bowl yields half the calories and allows you to eat more, which will keep you full longer. Now you can have a large bowl of warm awesomeness to start your day. This bowl is so good, I sometimes fix it for dessert.

- 1 cup baked spaghetti squash (from Prep Day page 120)
- 1 cup unsweetened almond milk or milk of your choice
- ½ cup instant oats
- 2 dashes cinnamon
- 2 teaspoons sweetener of your choice (honey, maple syrup, or brown sugar)

Optional Toppings: ¼ cup raisins, ¼ cup sunflower seeds or chopped nuts, or 1 scoop protein power

To get the most of your squash–use a fork or spoon to scrape out as much flesh as possible down to the clean shell. Place the spaghetti squash in a bowl; use a knife and fork directly in the bowl to cut it into bite-size pieces.

Add the almond milk and oats; mix well to combine.

Microwave 2 to 3 minutes to desired thickness, or heat on the stove in a small pot over medium heat, until bubbling.

Add the cinnamon and sweetener. Stir, taste, and adjust flavorings. Add your favorite toppings.

Tip: Make this the night before: Place all ingredients in a bowl, cover with plastic wrap, and refrigerate. In the morning, microwave 2 minutes, and enjoy. You really can't mess this one up.

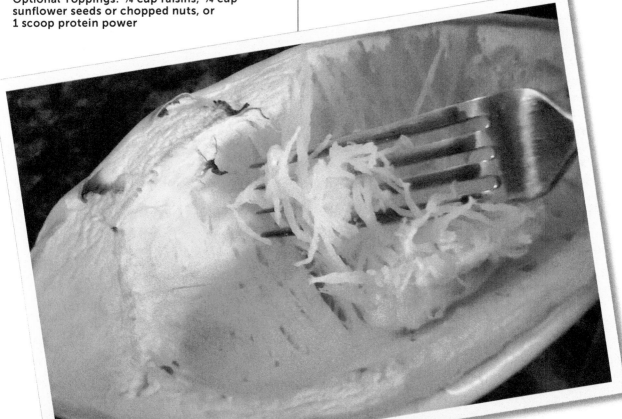

BREAKFAST

Smoothies

Total Time: 7 minutes · Serves: 1

Smoothies are not only delicious, but depending on what you add, they can serve as an entire meal. A smoothie is an excellent way to get yummy raw nutrients into the body quickly. If you have a hand immersion blender you can whip these up in minutes and only have one part to clean instead of an entire blender.

Below are just some guidelines for smoothies; go forth and experiment. Some turn out awesome and some need a little taste-and-adjust. To repair a smoothie-gone-*eh*, try a little more banana, fresh ginger, or a drop of vanilla extract. When I say a small fresh ginger nub, think roughly the size of a large grape.

Smoothies require a liquid in order for them to be pureed. If you do not have almond milk, simply use water, or a combination of ½ cup plain full-fat Greek yogurt and ½ cup water. Add liquid until you get the consistency you are in the mood for. Sometimes I want a thick creamy smoothie, and other days, I want more of a hearty juice drink.

Give your bod the best opportunity to absorb nutrients by remembering to combine a fat, protein, and carb in each smoothie.

You will need a hand immersion blender, food processor or blender.

Fruit

½ banana
¾ cup frozen berries
10 raw almonds or cashews
1 cup liquid (almond milk, water, or a combination of yogurt and water)
1 scoop vanilla protein powder

Chocolate Peanut Butter

½ banana
1 tablespoon cocoa powder, unsweetened
2 tablespoons peanut butter
1 cup liquid (almond milk, water, or a combination of yogurt and water)
1 scoop vanilla protein powder

Berry Green

½ banana or avocado
¾ cup frozen berries
1 cup fresh baby spinach
Nub of fresh ginger, peeled and roughly chopped, or generous dashes ground ginger
1 cup liquid (almond milk, water, or a combination of yogurt and water)
1 scoop vanilla protein powder

Cinnamon Chai

1 chai tea bag steeped in 1 cup hot water, discard tea bag after steeping
1 teaspoon honey, dissolved in the hot tea
Small nub of fresh ginger, peeled and roughly chopped, or 2 dashes ground ginger
3 dashes cinnamon
10 raw almonds or cashews
3-4 ice cubes
1-1½ cups liquid (almond milk, water, or a combination of yogurt and water)
1 scoop vanilla protein powder

Chocolate Lover

½ banana or avocado
1 cup fresh baby spinach
1 tablespoon cocoa powder, unsweetened
10 whole almonds
1 dash cayenne pepper
2 drops vanilla extract
2 ice cubes
1 cup liquid (almond milk, water, or a combination of yogurt and water)
1 scoop vanilla protein powder

Place the ingredients of your choice in a deep vessel like a 32-ounce yogurt container, and puree with a hand immersion blender until smooth. Pour into a glass and enjoy.

If you don't have a hand immersion blender, place the ingredients in a food processor or blender and process until smooth.

I build my smoothie in a glass jar, hit it with my hand immersion blender, screw on the lid, and I'm in the car. See ya!

Tip

Bananas going brown? Peel them, break them in half and place in a large plastic bag and toss in the freezer. I always have a bag of these waiting in my freezer because they make frothy ice cream-like smoothies. And sometimes a frozen banana makes a perfect dessert!

Malia's En*lightened* "Eggs Benedict"

Total Time: 30 minutes · Serves: 2

Okay people! Deep breath. We aren't poaching eggs and we aren't slathering on hollandaise sauce on this "Eggs Benedict." This light and modern twist will impress your mouth and your guests!

Spinach:

1 (8-ounce) bag large-leaf spinach
Salt
Pepper
Red pepper flakes
Juice from 1-2 lemon wedges (⅙ to ⅓ lemon)

Eggs:

2 teaspoons extra virgin olive oil
4 eggs
Salt
Pepper

Assembly:

Freshly baked French baguette
4 slices prosciutto
Extra virgin olive oil
Oregano
Red pepper flakes

Prosciutto is ham that has been salt-cured and air-dried. For more on Prosciutto, see page 150.

"Not having tried something before is a very good reason to try it now."
Melissa Kelly, executive chef of Primo Restaurant

BREAKFAST

Spinach:

Heat a large nonstick frying pan over medium heat; add ¼ cup water. Once steam rises off the water, add the entire bag of spinach, tearing the leaves as you go. Remove massive stems; but don't fuss too much, it will cook down. Cover, and allow to steam for only 2 minutes. Spinach just needs to wilt, so refrain from overcooking this green. Add dashes of salt, pepper, and red pepper flakes. Drizzle lemon juice over, and toss. Set aside in a bowl, juices and all.

Eggs:

Return the same frying pan (no need to wash) to medium heat. Add the oil, and heat about 2 minutes. Once the oil is hot, crack in 2 eggs. Sprinkle with salt and pepper.

Cook sunny side up until whites are cooked through. If you prefer your egg over-easy, gently flip the egg, and cook the other side just 20 seconds to ensure the whites are cooked. Do not overcook; you want the yolks to be runny. Repeat with the next set of eggs.

Assembly:

While eggs are cooking, use a serrated knife to cut four 1-inch slices from the baguette.

Place two slices on each of the two plates. Top the baguette with sautéed spinach. You can squeeze out a little juice from the spinach if you don't want your bread too soggy. I like it soggy, and the spinach juice adds flavor and nutrients!

Carefully place the fried eggs on top of the spinach.

Lift the bread, and wrap a thin piece of prosciutto entirely around each Benedict. Drizzle each with olive oil and garnish with generous amounts of oregano and red pepper flakes.

Smile and serve!

Pasta Salad

LUNCH

Total Time: 25 minutes· Serves: 4-5

Pasta salad is a great thing to have awaiting you when you peer into the fridge. There is no set recipe for pasta salad as everyone has a preference derived from childhood. Some people like a creamy pasta salad, while others enjoy a zesty pasta salad. Some people like spiral pasta, while others like elbows, bow ties, or penne. The successful recipe is whatever tastes good to you! This is what makes pasta salad versatile and exciting, yielding a different outcome each time, depending on what ingredients you have on hand. Just keep tasting and adding. Now go use up those veggies!

- 2 teaspoons salt
- 2 cups whole wheat spirals or elbows
- ½ cup chopped red or green bell peppers
- ½ cup chopped zucchini
- ½ cup chopped summer squash
- 1 cup finely chopped celery
- ¼ cup chopped red onions
- 2 carrots, shredded or peeled into ribbons with a peeler
- ½ pint grape tomatoes, halved
- ½ teaspoon salt
- ¼ teaspoon pepper
- ¼ teaspoon red pepper flakes
- 1 teaspoon dried oregano
- 1 teaspoon dried basil, thyme, or marjoram
- 1-2 teaspoons Braggs Liquid Aminos
- Optional Ingredients: 2 tablespoons capers with juice; fresh herbs; ½ cup frozen peas, thawed in warm water and drained; canned tuna, drained; canned chickpeas, rinsed well and drained

Dressing Options:

For Creamy Pasta Salad:

- 2-3 tablespoons plain full-fat Greek yogurt
- 1 tablespoon extra virgin olive oil

or

For Zesty Pasta Salad:

- 1-2 tablespoons vinegar of your choice (apple cider or balsamic)
- 1-2 tablespoons extra virgin olive oil

Fill a medium pot halfway with cold water, add the salt. Bring to a boil over high heat, about 5 minutes.

Once boiling, reduce heat to medium. Add the pasta, stir, and cook for 5 minutes. Do not overcook, or the pasta salad will be mushy. Pasta should be a little firm to the bite (al dente).

Drain the pasta (I just tip the pot over sink, holding back noodles with a spatula. One less strainer to clean right?) Rinse under cold water to stop the cooking process. Drain well.

Place the pasta in a large bowl, add peppers, zucchini, summer squash, celery, onions, carrots, tomatoes, salt, pepper, red pepper flakes, oregano, basil, and Braggs. Add optional ingredients if you like. Gently stir to combine without crushing the tomatoes.

Mix the ingredients of either the Creamy or the Zesty dressing together in a small bowl, and add dressing to the pasta salad; toss well.

Taste and add more dressing and salt to your liking.

Enjoy now or cover and refrigerate allowing flavors to blend. Use within 5 days.

Food for Thought:

What was your best experience cooking through Food That Works?

I'd love to hear your story! Write me: malia@foodthatworks.info

DINNER

Tuna Melt

Total Time: 15 minutes · Makes: 1 large Tuna Melt

When you're tired, hungry, and in no mood to cook, nothing quite hits the spot like a warm Tuna Melt. This recipe makes one large Tuna Melt. But it can also be cut in half and accompanied with a side salad to create a nice lunch for two. Greek yogurt is used here as a healthful substitution for mayonnaise. Chopped celery adds a delicious fresh crunch to tuna fish. Not only is it a good way to use up that celery you bought last week, but it serves as a filler to make your tuna fish go further. Try to tuck in as many veggies as possible to increase your veggie-to-meat ratio, and get more bang for your buck. Whole wheat tortillas are also a healthful alternative because they have fewer ingredients, calories, and carbs than bread.

Experiment with your tuna fish by adding extras like fresh dill, chopped peppers, sliced scallions, capers, hot sauce, pickles, pepperoncini, hot pepper relish, grapes, or sliced apples.

1 can best quality tuna, drained
2 tablespoons plain full-fat Greek yogurt
½ cup finely chopped celery (if you have it)
¼ cup finely chopped red onions
Salt
Pepper
1 large whole wheat flour tortilla
¼ cup shredded sharp Cheddar cheese
Hot sauce (optional)

Place the tuna fish in a medium bowl. Add the yogurt, celery, onions. Taste, and add optional ingredients of your choice; season with salt and pepper to your liking.

Place a large nonstick frying pan over medium heat. Put the tortilla directly in the hot pan, no oil necessary. Sprinkle the cheese around entire tortilla. Spoon a generous amount of the tuna mixture onto one side of the tortilla. Cook until cheese is melted, and tuna is warm, about 2 minutes. Fold in half (like a quesadilla). Press down with a spatula. Flipping once, cook until both sides are golden brown, about 1 minute on each side.

Serve with hot sauce and a side of Mixed Salad.

DINNER

Sweet Potato Quesadillas with Quick Salsa

Prep Time: 30 minutes · Serves: 2

Sound crazy? Wait until you try this delicious spin on the ol' familiar quesadilla. This recipe was adapted from one my *favorite* restaurants in Watertown Massachusetts, The Red Lentil.

Sweet Potato:

1 large sweet potato, peeled, cut into ½-inch cubes
1 teaspoon extra virgin olive oil
2 dashes ground cumin
2 dashes cayenne pepper
Salt
Pepper

Asparagus:

1 bunch asparagus, chopped in 1-inch pieces (see Prep Day page 120)
1 teaspoon extra virgin olive oil
½ teaspoon Braggs Liquid Aminos or ¼ teaspoon salt
2 dashes pepper
2 lemon wedges (⅓ lemon)

Assembly:

2 large whole wheat flour tortillas
½ cup shredded sharp Cheddar cheese
4 scallions, light green and white parts, thinly sliced
½ cup Quick Salsa (from Prep Day page 122)

For Dipping:

4 tablespoons plain full-fat Greek yogurt
Hot sauce

Preheat oven to Bake 350°F. Position one oven rack at the top, closest to the heat source, and the other rack in the middle. Line a large baking sheet with tin foil.

Sweet Potato:

Place the sweet potatoes in a large bowl. Add the olive oil, cumin, and cayenne. Season with salt and pepper. Stir with a spoon to coat the sweet potatoes. Spread the seasoned potatoes onto the prepared baking sheet, place in the oven on the middle rack. Bake for 15 minutes, set timer.

Asparagus:

Place the asparagus in the same large bowl. Add the olive oil, Braggs, and pepper. Squeeze the juice from the lemon wedges on top. Stir with a spoon to coat the asparagus.

Once timer for the potatoes goes off, set the oven to Broil–High.

Use a spatula to move the sweet potatoes over to one side of the baking sheet, making room for the asparagus. Arrange the asparagus in one flat layer next to the sweet potatoes. Place in the oven on the top rack so that the veggies are about 2 inches from the heat source; leave door ajar. Broil for 6 to 8 minutes, and check often as the asparagus broil *really* fast. Once the potatoes and asparagus are nicely charred, remove from oven, and turn oven off.

Assembly:

Place a large nonstick frying pan over medium heat. Put a tortilla directly in the hot pan, no oil necessary. Sprinkle ¼ cup cheese over the entire tortilla.

Spoon generous amounts of sweet potatoes and asparagus onto one side of the tortilla, leave 1 inch of space from the edge so the ingredients don't fall out.

Add scallions and spoonfuls of Quick Salsa.

Fold in half, and press down with a spatula. Cover the pan with the lid, and cook for 5 minutes. Flipping once, cook until both sides are golden brown, about 1 minute on each side.

Repeat with the second quesadilla.

Serve on a plate with yogurt and hot sauce.

Tip
Keep any extra charbroiled asparagus and sweet potatoes in the fridge and use cold on top of salads throughout the week.

Southwestern Baked Mac and Cheese

Prep Time: 30 minutes · Cook Time: 20 minutes
Serves: 6

Try this mature twist to liven up traditional mac and cheese. By making it yourself, you can make it healthful! The cumin, peppers, and onions give this dish a distinct Southwestern flair. Go on back for seconds because this dish has more vegetables than pasta. *Shhh!* Serve a portion of this warm deliciousness with a side salad for an exceptionally colorful plate.

Cheese Sauce:

4 tablespoons (½ stick) unsalted butter
¼ cup flour
2 cups unsweetened almond milk or milk of your choice
1½ cups shredded sharp Cheddar cheese, divided
½ teaspoon ground cumin
¼ teaspoon cayenne pepper
3 teaspoons hot sauce, divided
1 teaspoon salt
¼ teaspoon black pepper
Optional: dashes of turmeric and paprika for color

1 teaspoon safflower oil or extra virgin olive oil, to grease baking dish

Assembly:

2 teaspoons salt
3 cups (half of a 16-ounce bag) whole wheat spirals or elbows
1 cup chopped zucchini
1 cup chopped summer squash
1 cup chopped yellow onions
1 cup chopped green bell peppers
½ cup chopped red bell peppers

Cheese Sauce:

First, create a roux: Melt the butter in a large nonstick frying pan over medium heat. With a whisk, slowly add the flour to the butter. Keep breaking up the flour with the whisk, pressing up against and scraping the sides.

Whisk while slowly adding 1 cup almond milk. Turn the heat up to high, and whisk continually until the sauce bubbles, thickens, and turns white. Add the remaining 1 cup almond milk; whisking another 2 minutes until the mixture bubbles and thickens again. Turn heat off but leave pan on the warm burner.

Add 1 cup cheese, the cumin, cayenne, 1 teaspoon hot sauce, salt, and pepper. Stir until cheese is melted. Taste. Add more spices if desired. If you want your mac and cheese to be a nice orange color add generous dashes of turmeric and paprika to your cheese sauce!

Preheat the oven to Bake 350°F. Grease a large glass or ceramic baking dish with oil, spread with your hands or a paper towel to coat all surfaces.

Assembly:

Fill a large pot halfway with cold water, add the salt. Bring to a boil over high heat, about 5 minutes. Once boiling, reduce heat to medium. Add the pasta; stir. Set timer for 3 minutes exactly. Do not overcook pasta, it will get fully cooked in the oven.

Drain pasta, and return to the same pot. Quickly add the zucchini, squash, onions, and peppers to the pot of pasta and pour in the cheese sauce. With a large spoon, gently combine, trying not to mush the pasta too much.

Pour the mac and cheese into the prepared baking dish. Sprinkle the top with the remaining ½ cup shredded cheese and the remaining 2 teaspoons hot sauce; this makes the top nice and crispy.

Bake until the top is golden brown, about 20 minutes.

Serve with a side of Mixed Salad with toppings of your choice.

Tip

Make two! This dish freezes well, so I always bake it in two separate dishes. One for instant gratification; the other, I cool completely, wrap three times with tin foil, and freeze for later in the week when I don't feel like cooking. Just remove the foil, and place the frozen dish directly into the oven at 350°F until hot in the center, about 30 minutes. Once you taste this creation, you will understand why people ask for it again and again.

DINNER

Turkey Meatballs with Robust Tomato Sauce over Spaghetti Squash

Total Time: 1 hour and 15 minutes · Serves: 4-5

Get ready for this thick, robust tomato sauce kissed with red wine. This sauce has big flavor you can achieve only with time, patience, and a whole lot of tasting along the way.

I serve my meatballs on spaghetti squash so I don't get that super-full tired feeling I get after eating pasta. Spaghetti squash has very few calories (42 calories in 1 cup), so swap out a cup of pasta for a cup of spaghetti squash, and you've got yourself a low-calorie, low-carb meal! You don't have to omit pasta every time, but give spaghetti squash a try at least once, so you can experience the versatility of this incredible vegetable.

Some days, you just need a big comforting, bowl of thick sauce and meatballs in your life. Let this recipe be your remedy.

Tomato Sauce:

2 tablespoons extra virgin olive oil

1 cup chopped yellow onions

4 cloves garlic, finely chopped

1 (28-ounce) can whole plum tomatoes, with juice

¼ cup red wine (optional)

2 bay leaves (if you have them)

½ teaspoon dried sage

½ teaspoon dried thyme

¼ teaspoon pepper

1½ teaspoons salt

1 teaspoon dried oregano

1 teaspoon dried basil

1 dash red pepper flakes

Meatballs:

¾ cup chopped green bell peppers

¾ cup chopped yellow onions

1 pound ground turkey

4 cloves garlic, finely chopped

1 cup instant oats

2 tablespoons Worcestershire sauce

2 tablespoons Braggs Liquid Aminos or
   1 tablespoon low-sodium soy sauce

1 teaspoon dried oregano

½ teaspoon dried thyme

1 teaspoon fennel seeds, crushed in fingers

½ teaspoon salt

¼ teaspoon pepper

3 tablespoons safflower oil, for frying

Assembly:

4 cups baked spaghetti squash (from Prep Day
   page 120)

Tomato Sauce:

Heat the olive oil in a large pot over medium-high heat. Once the oil is hot, add the onions, and garlic. Sauté about 5 minutes, stirring frequently.

Roughly chop the canned tomatoes into large chunks (no need to be fussy they will all turn into sauce in the end). Add the tomatoes with juice, ½ cup water, wine, and bay leaves to pot; stir. Allow to bubble and cook until sauce starts to thicken, about 10 minutes. Stir in the sage, thyme, pepper, salt, oregano, basil, and red pepper flakes.

Reduce the heat to low, and keep warm until ready to serve, stirring occasionally. You want the sauce to cook down and become concentrated. If it gets too thick, add splashes of wine or water to thin it to a desired consistency; stir. Remove and discard the bay leaves. If you like your sauce smooth versus chunky, transfer the sauce to a deep bowl, and puree it with a hand immersion blender to desired texture.

Meatballs:

Take a second to finely chop the chopped peppers and onions into smaller bits. Just mow over them with a chef's knife several times; this will help the meatballs stay together better.

In a large bowl, place the turkey, garlic, onions, peppers, oats, Worcestershire sauce, Braggs, oregano, thyme, fennel, salt, and pepper. With your hands, gently fold and combine ingredients, trying not to mush or mess with the mixture too much or the meatballs will be overworked and tough. I know you want to, but refrain from squeezing the meat through your fingers. If the mixture is too wet, sprinkle in a little more oats until you can form balls. There are a lot of veggies in the mix; do your best to get a good meat-to-veggie ratio in each ball, and mold the meat around the veggies so they hold together and don't fall apart when frying. Pack and shape equal-size balls.

Heat the safflower oil in a large nonstick frying pan over medium-high heat. Once the oil is hot, carefully add the meatballs. Meatballs should sizzle when they hit the oil. Once one side is well browned, use a fork and spoon to turn them gently, one by one, so they do not fall apart. Cook until all sides are browned, about 10 to 12 minutes.

Once the meatballs are fully brown, turn heat to low, and cook another 5 to 10 minutes, turning them often. Cut one meatball in half to ensure center is cooked through. The center should not be raw or pink; poultry must be fully cooked. The entire meatball should be one solid color, firm, and juicy. If still wet or pink in middle, cook another 5 minutes. Remove meatballs and place on the side, or you can add them directly to the tomato sauce.

Assembly:

Scrape the baked spaghetti squash into stringy shreds with a fork. Use a spoon to scrape out as much flesh as possible down to the clean shell. Place into a medium pot with ¼ cup water. Cover, and heat over medium-high heat until squash is hot, about 5 minutes. Drain.

Plate the spaghetti squash, and top with meatballs and sauce. *Buon Appetito!*

LEFTOVERS:

Pack leftovers for lunch tomorrow. Damn right, this meal gets even better the second time around!

If you need to use up the rest of that baguette from the Eggs Benedict recipe, then tuck leftover meatballs into a sub or make Garlic Bread (page 137).

Black Bean Spinach Enchilada Bake

Prep Time: 35 minutes · Cook Time: 25 minutes
Serves: 4-6

This enchilada is bursting with clean fresh flavor and is super light since it is full of veggies. This dish will have everyone going up for seconds! *Olé!*

Don't already love beans? Learn to. I could write an entire book solely on beans, their nutritional benefits, and the millions of dishes you can make with them. There are so many varieties, you are bound to find one that you like and that agrees with your stomach. This book is all about substituting ingredients, so make it work for you! Go get your bean on!

Spinach:

½ cup chopped yellow onions
1 (8-ounce) bag large-leaf spinach
Juice from 3 lime wedges (½ lime)
Salt
Pepper

Corn and Bean Mixture:

1 (15-ounce) can corn, rinsed well and drained
1 (15-ounce) can black beans, rinsed well and drained
½ bunch fresh cilantro leaves, chopped
½ teaspoon ground cumin
½ teaspoon chili powder
¼ teaspoon cayenne pepper
½ teaspoon Braggs Liquid Aminos or ¼ teaspoon salt
Juice from 3 lime wedges (½ lime)

Assembly:

8 small corn tortillas, torn into 2-inch pieces
1 cup chopped green bell peppers
1 cup chopped zucchini
1 cup chopped summer squash
2 cups cottage cheese
½ cup shredded sharp Cheddar cheese
2 (4-ounce) cans diced green chiles

Serve With:
Quick Salsa (from Prep Day page 122) and hot sauce

Preheat oven to Bake 400°F. Position a rack in the middle of the oven.

Spinach:

Place a large nonstick frying pan with a lid over medium-high heat; add ¼ cup water. Once steam rises off the water, add the onions and entire bag of spinach, tearing the leaves as you go. Cover and steam for 3 minutes. Remove from heat. Squeeze in lime juice, season with salt and pepper, and set aside.

Corn and Bean Mixture:

In a medium mixing bowl, combine the corn, black beans, cilantro, cumin, chili powder, cayenne, and Braggs. Squeeze lime juice into the mixture, gently stir, and set aside.

Assembly:

In a large baking dish, evenly distribute the ingredients below.

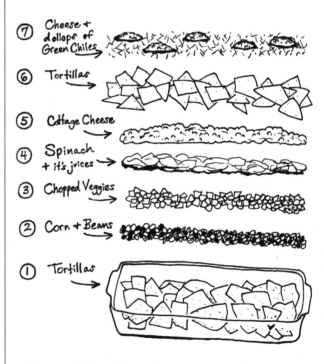

⑦ Cheese + dollops of Green Chiles
⑥ Tortillas
⑤ Cottage Cheese
④ Spinach + it's juices
③ Chopped Veggies
② Corn + Beans
① Tortillas

Tap the baking dish on the countertop a few times to gently pack layers together.

Bake until heated through, about 25 minutes; set timer.

Cut into squares, and serve with Quick Salsa and hot sauce.

Baked Sweet Potatoes

Total Time: 3 minutes

Keeping baked sweet potatoes on hand in my fridge is one of my best discoveries. When I am hungry for a snack, I find myself biting into these cold, like an apple, skin and all. They are sweet, smooth, and very satisfying. Always remember to add a little bit of fat–a pat of butter, coconut oil, or drizzle of olive oil–so you can best absorb the fat-soluble nutrients in this scrumptious vegetable.

If you did not bake sweet potatoes in advance, it takes about 1 hour, see Prep Day page 120.

Try these options:

- Chop them up and add them cold to salads.

- Highlight their sweet side with dried cranberries, cinnamon, or maple syrup.

- Top them with a dollop of yogurt, some scallions, salt, and pepper.

- Simply mash them with butter, salt, and pepper.

- Quickly reheat them in the microwave to accompany any meal.

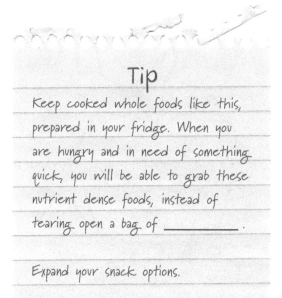

Tip

Keep cooked whole foods like this, prepared in your fridge. When you are hungry and in need of something quick, you will be able to grab these nutrient dense foods, instead of tearing open a bag of _____ .

Expand your snack options.

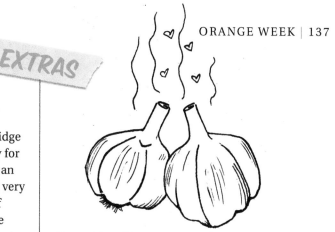

EXTRAS

Garlic Bread

Prep Time: 10 minutes · Cook Time: 10 minutes

If you have any leftover French baguette that needs to be used up, garlic bread is a great option. If the bread is going stale, you can revive it for this recipe by sprinkling a little water onto the bread before you add toppings and put it in the oven. You can halve or double this recipe depending on how much garlic bread you want to make, this is just a rough guide.

1 (12-inch) piece French baguette
2 tablespoons extra virgin olive oil
2 tablespoons mayonnaise or unsalted butter, at room temperature (optional)
2-3 cloves garlic, peeled and finely chopped
1 teaspoon dried basil
1 teaspoon dried oregano
¼ teaspoon salt

Preheat oven to Bake 400°F. Position a rack in the middle of the oven. Line a large baking sheet with tin foil for easy clean up.

Slice the baguette in half lengthwise, and lay the two halves, cut-side up, on the prepared baking sheet. If the bread is stale, sprinkle it with splashes of water with your fingertips.

In a small bowl, combine the olive oil, mayonnaise, garlic, basil, oregano, and salt; making a paste.

Use a knife to spread the paste evenly all over the cut sides of the bread.

For soft garlic bread, fold the tin foil over the bread to make a sealed pouch. For crispy garlic bread, leave the bread uncovered.

Bake until the bread is golden brown, about 10 minutes.

Morning Glory Muffins

Prep Time: 20 minutes · Cook Time: 35 minutes
Makes: 12 muffins

This is a healthful snack when you are craving baked goods. It's quick and easy to whip up, and is a great recipe to use up leftover carrots and zucchini.

1 teaspoon safflower oil to grease pan

Dry Ingredients:
1½ cups flour
1 cup instant oats
1½ teaspoons baking powder
1½ teaspoons ground cinnamon
½ teaspoon ground ginger
½ teaspoon salt

Wet Ingredients:
1 banana
¾ cup packed brown sugar
2 tablespoons safflower oil
1 cup plain full-fat Greek yogurt
1 teaspoon vanilla extract
1 egg
1 tablespoon black strap molasses (if you have it)
1 cup shredded zucchini
1½ cups shredded carrots
½ cup raisins
½ cup raw sunflower seeds or chopped nuts

Preheat oven to Bake 350°F. Position a rack in the middle of the oven.

Grease a muffin tin or shallow baking dish with oil, spread with your hands or a paper towel to coat all surfaces.

In a large bowl, combine the flour, oats, baking powder, cinnamon, ginger, and salt.

In a medium bowl, mash up the banana with a fork. Add the brown sugar, oil, yogurt, vanilla, egg, and molasses. Mix well until smooth. Stir in the zucchini and carrots.

Pour the wet mixture into the dry. Gently fold to combine, but do not overmix or muffins will be tough. Add the raisins and seeds; stir once.

Spoon the batter into the greased muffin tin, filling each hole three-quarters full.

Bake until a toothpick inserted in the centers of the muffins comes out clean, about 25 to 28 minutes.

Cool completely on a wire rack.

HIGH FIVE!

Thank You

I want to thank some special people who have deeply influenced my life and the creation of this book. I am forever indebted to you and incredibly grateful our paths have crossed. Thank you.

Jim–for generously providing me with a funky artist lab to give birth to this book. I seriously couldn't have done it without you.

Ruth–for leaving behind a treasure trove of loving artifacts and cookbooks. Although I never had the honor to meet you, you were the inspiration for much of the design of this book.

Melissa–for showing me what hard work is and for teaching me to respectfully slaughter and butcher animals. I am now confident I will survive the zombie apocalypse.

Hector–for my famous ceramic to-go teacup and for letting us tattoo you that night

Andrea–for teaching me the secret, "vivir la vida hermosa y sin vergüenza"

Casandra & Deb–for being my original motivation to create this book

Emily–for getting me addicted to tea in college

Joshua–for teaching me how to cook when I was twenty-three years old

Renée–for teaching me to buy used, create less waste, and be a conscious consumer. You were doing this way before it was "cool." I must admit, you ignited my romance with frugal living, which sparked my evolution to become the gypsy I am today.

Trelawney–for teaching me to indulge in, absorb, and relish life

Sophie–for being my tenacious cheerleader who never let me quit

Anna–for continuously preaching to me about balance, even though I am still searching for it myself

Ayse & Cengiz–for welcoming me like family into your farm-to-table existence. Living with you in the Dikencik Cottages in Turkey changed my life.

Hillary & Mirek of Camden Design–for designing this extraordinary book

Uncle Richard & Suzanne–for inspiring me to go to Turkey. You were right.

Will–for your unfailing support and our shared love of Chris Farley

Rene, Pernille, Peter, Johanna, Esben–for being my Danish family

Paula & Sheilah of Cookbook Construction Crew–for agreeing to work with a novice like me. You were extremely thorough and a joy to work with. Can we still talk?

Stephen–for all your loving support and assistance

Taylor–for your fine techspertise, building my website, managing my social media and developing a killer marketing strategy

Annie–for keeping me physically strong and sane

Aunt Helen–for your thorough testing and feedback

Nicole–for being my precious friend and for filming my Kickstarter video

Shelly–for being the most efficient, dependable, considerate person I know. I strive to be like you.

Nicole & Christine–for being my foundation

Jacinda–for your spirit, support, and ambitious photo shoots

Al–for being a kickass self-taught yoga teacher. You are living proof of my credo that, in certain instances, one's passion can outweigh any certification.

Judith–for your unending generosity

Dave–for the long hours shooting my food and doing so beautifully.

Nicole–for sticking through the painful sessions of proofreading. You are dependable, strong, and talented beyond words.

Leo–for patiently teaching me Spanish (Sorry that one had nothing to do with the book.)

Carrie–for fabricating the most beautiful handmade vintage *CarrieSewFancy* aprons for me

Galen–for being my big bro, from the womb to the tomb! I love you.

Sandy–for being my mentor, guru, and holistic healer. I am in awe of everything you do.

Dad–for pushing me and for being my biggest critic. Your creative brain amazes me more every single day. I am so proud to be your daughter.

Michael–for introducing me to the minimalist lifestyle

Cori & Randy–for creating *Backyard Brine Pickle Co.*, the greatest pickles on EARTH

Mom–for always being there for me, and for teaching me "to want something more than my fear is holding me back from getting." You have given me wings.

The Universe–for being so amazing. For introducing me to all these people. And teaching me to trust.

INGREDIENTS GUIDE

This Ingredients Guide is intended to help you make the best choices at the grocery store. It helps you locate ingredients and explains certain items. It offers *examples* of what to look for on the ingredients labels to help you compare brands. It teaches you how to select the best quality products and produce and tells you why it is important to buy certain items organic versus commercial. This guide offers healthful substitutions, explains why I chose the ingredients I did, and provides a few other notes, as if I were shopping alongside you. There will be some new items introduced to your cart, so refer to this Guide if you have any questions along the way.

Asterisk (*) suggests to buy organic

Almond Butter

Avoid brands with added sugar or oil. Almond butter is a good substitute for peanut butter. Benefits: excellent source of healthful fat and protein, rich in antioxidants, supports bone health, promotes heart health.

Almond Milk

Select brands that are unsweetened, like Blue Diamond. This is a good option for people with dairy sensitivities. Almond milk can be used in any recipe to replace milk.

Apple Cider Vinegar

Select quality unfiltered apple cider vinegar. It will appear cloudy because it contains strands of proteins, enzymes, and friendly bacteria. Benefits: good source of probiotics, aids in digestion, promotes gut health, also believed to support immune function, and possibly increase energy.

Asian Noodles

Pad Thai noodles are made with rice flour and resemble flat spaghetti. These noodles are common in stir-fries and street food in Thailand. Any Asian noodle can be substituted in the Peanut Pad Thai recipe (page 110), so experiment with the different types located in the Asian section. Try Soba noodles (buckwheat flour), or Udon noodles (wheat flour); you can even use angel hair pasta, preferably whole wheat.

Avocado

Avocados have a small window of being perfectly ripe and are one of those foods you must select carefully, with a plan in mind of when you will use them. Quicken the ripening process by storing them in a closed paper bag; slow down the ripening process by storing them in the refrigerator. Benefits: excellent source of healthful fat, good source of potassium, promotes heart health, regulates blood pressure.
Underripe: The skin is bright green and the avocado is rock hard, does not give when squeezed.
Ripe: The skin is dark green or black. The skin should give a little when squeezed.
Overripe: The skin is black and has sunken spots. They are mushy or have uneven soft spots when squeezed.

Baked Goods

Commercially sold baked goods tend to have a lot of

added ingredients to retain texture and avoid spoilage. This makes it difficult to find baked goods with fewer than ten listed ingredients. Select baked goods that say, "100% whole grain." Whatever type of whole grain that might be, wheat, quinoa, barley, or rice, make sure it is the first listed ingredient on the list, and not listed seven items down! As always, select the one with the fewest listed ingredients.

Beans

Select brands that are reduced sodium and are free of additional preservatives or firming agents. Canned beans are a great option for busy people. I suggest keeping your pantry stocked with a variety of canned beans for quick impromptu dinners. They are inexpensive, filling, and make a great replacement for meat. They can be eaten warm or cold, added to soups and salads, or pureed into dips. In recipes calling for beans, almost any bean will do, so feel free to substitute. Did you know that beans can be a mood enhancer? They are good sources of tryptophan, which is known to increase serotonin levels, which can ward off depression. Important: when using canned beans, always drain and rinse them well to remove the liquid, which contains sugars and starches that can disrupt the stomach. Also, rinsing canned food reduces sodium by about 40 percent. Benefits: excellent source of protein, rich in antioxidants and magnesium, low in fat, promotes heart and colon health.

Braggs Liquid Aminos

Braggs is a condiment that contains amino acids and tastes similar to soy sauce. I use Braggs for flavoring and salting foods. If you don't have Braggs, you can substitute low-sodium soy sauce or salt to taste.

Butter

Select unsalted, high quality butter to reap its healthful benefits. To ensure butter was made from quality milk, look for words like "pasture-fed" or "grass-fed." Quality butter has a rich golden color passed on from the grass the cows ate versus the white waxy appearance of butter from grain-fed cows. By all means, avoid margarines or vegetable spreads if you value your health! The best quality butter is sometimes located in the specialty cheese section, see brands like Kerrygold.

Cauliflower

This versatile veggie can be eaten raw or cooked. Raw, it adds a surprisingly nutty crunch to salads. Steam it for a side dish, puree it into soups, or mash it with potatoes–delicious. Cauliflower, along with broccoli, kale, Brussels sprouts, and cabbage, is a cruciferous vegetable, which promotes liver health. A healthy liver is the first step to losing weight, since the liver manages the delegation of fat. Cauliflower is packed with vitamin C; one cup of cauliflower contains almost as much vitamin C as an orange! Do not be intimidated by cauliflower; it is very forgiving and almost impossible to mess up. Benefits: low in calories; high in fiber; excellent source of vitamins C and K, potassium, and magnesium.

Cheese

Select quality cheese from the specialty cheese section. Real cheese has only four or five ingredients in it. Flip over that lame bag of shredded cheese, and you will see the weird stuff they have added to it, including anticaking and antimold agents. Bleck! You are in the wrong aisle, buddy. Do your taste buds a favor, and go buy a quality block of cheese with some real frickin' flavor. Grate it yourself, and enjoy delicious cheese all week.

*Chicken Breasts

Select the best quality chicken available. Look for words like "no hormones," "no antibiotics," "vegetarian-fed," "pasture-raised," "free-range," and "local." Chicken breasts are the most convenient cut for beginner cooks, and they are easy to prepare and store. Keeping baked chicken breasts ready in the fridge makes it a breeze to assemble the meals you would typically order out!

Chicken Broth

Select broth that is low-sodium and organic. Broth sold in cartons tends to have less salt than broth in cans, as the canning process requires additional

salt. Homemade bone broth is superior because it is extremely nutritious and offers amazing healing qualities. Broths are the bases for nutritious cooking around the world. Restaurants have huge stockpots boiling at all times. I suggest referencing Sally Fallon's *Nourishing Traditions,* for more information on making your own broths, definitely something I recommend getting into. It is extremely easy and since you will be cooking more, you will have lots of good vegetable scraps you can store in a bag in the freezer and use to flavor future broths.

Chipotle Peppers in Adobo

Chipotle peppers are ripe red jalapeño peppers which have been smoke-dried and then canned in a Spanish sauce called adobo. The smoking process creates a distinctive smokey flavor. Chipotle peppers are quite hot and should be added gradually to a recipe, tasted, and then increased if you want more heat. Extra chipotle peppers can be saved by placing them in a plastic bag, removing the air, flattening them out, and freezing them. In the future, you can break off a piece, and add it to a recipe for flavor and spice.

Citrus Fruit

Select small citrus, with thin, soft skins; they typically are the juiciest. They should have a little give when you squeeze them. The juice is especially good on salads or leafy greens because it assists in the absorption of nutrients like vitamin K. Citrus is delicate and can lose vitamins when heated; it's best to add it at the end, after cooking is complete. Benefits: excellent source of vitamin C; good source of flavonoids, which provide anti-inflammatory properties; supports liver function.

Coconut Oil

Select cold-pressed, virgin, unrefined varieties. Coconut oil is one of the more stable oils; it can stand up to high heat and has a longer shelf life. I use coconut oil for most of my cooking, or I spread it on foods in place of butter because I love the flavor. Experiment and do what feels right to you, just know that coconut oil can always be substituted for oil or butter. Benefits: excellent source of healthful fat, has antibacterial properties, improves brain function, lowers blood cholesterol.

Cornmeal

Select stone ground varieties that are medium- or coarse-ground. "Stone-ground" cornmeal is less processed. It is a whole grain because it still has the hull and the oil-rich germ, which provide vitamins, minerals, and fiber. Cornmeal is incredibly versatile. It can be sweetened and used in corn bread or muffins, or eaten as porridge instead of oatmeal. It can be savory, made into polenta, which makes a great creamy substitute for pasta. Polenta is divine topped with red sauce or a couple fried eggs.

Cottage Cheese

Select plain cottage cheese. I recommend country style (large curd) for the Charbroiled Vegetable Lasagna (page 65), because it melts nicely. Try Hood *Chive* Cottage Cheese (small curd) for salads. If sodium is a concern for you, low-sodium varieties are available. Cottage cheese is a delicious healthful substitute for creamy salad dressing. Top a salad with a big dollop of cottage cheese–guilt free! Benefits: excellent source of protein and calcium, low in fat, filling.

Flour

For maximum health benefits, select whole wheat flour versus enriched white flour. Whole wheat flour still has its bran and germ intact, therefore it yields a little coarser texture and is tan in color. The bran and germ hold most of the wheat's valuable nutrients, minerals, and oils, and all of its fiber, making it a nutrient-rich whole food. Whole wheat flour still has its healthful oils, and natural oils can oxidize and go rancid quicker than people think. Therefore, it is important to store whole grain flour in a tightly sealed container in the refrigerator and use it in 3 to 6 months. Whole wheat flour does not last forever, as no real food should! On the other hand, enriched white flour has been processed and bleached in order to increase its shelf life and the shelf life of the products it is in, like pastas, breads, cookies, and baked goods. In white flour, the wheat bran and germ have been removed, therefore stripping it of its nutrients. The United States requires that some of these nutrients be replaced; that is why white flour is "enriched" with vitamins, meaning some were added back in, but it is still nutritionally inferior. Again, you have the information, make changes at your own pace, according to what is right for you.

Fruits

Fruits are crucial to our health. In addition to being rich sources of water-soluble vitamins that we need daily, they are the only foods that contain special enzymes that help aid in digestion. Besides their major health benefits, they are delicious. Fruit is an easy whole food because it is best consumed raw and requires little prep beyond cutting or peeling, making it a great portable snack for people on the go! Remember, the peel (skin) of fruits and vegetables tends to hold the highest concentration of nutrients and antioxidants, even more than the flesh, so you might as well splurge for organic and skip the peeling and loss of nutrients!

Garlic

For the best flavor, it is worth seeking out local organic varieties of garlic. There are over 400 different varieties of garlic out there to try, ranging from hot and strong to sweet and mild. In my opinion, the commercial garlic and "jumbo" garlic have no flavor. Garlic can be consumed raw to receive the most health benefits or cooked to reduce its pungency. A typical garlic bulb is made up of eight to twenty cloves. For instructions on peeling garlic, see page 20. Benefits: rich in antioxidants; good source of vitamin C; has anti-inflammatory properties; has antifungal and antiviral properties, which help to fight off the common cold; promotes detoxification; warms the body; supports immune system function; regulates blood pressure.

Ginger

Fresh ginger looks like a nubby root with shiny tan skin. Under the thin brown skin, ginger is yellow in color and has a distinct aroma that is spicy and sweet. It is an integral ingredient in Indian and Asian cuisines. It is sold by weight, so snap off a nice firm piece the size you need. It should break off cleanly and have a pungent smell. Avoid ginger that is soft, wrinkled, cracked, or dry. Always wash ginger well before using it. Ginger is great on fish, vegetables, in any rice dishes, curries, stir-fries, marinades, desserts, baked goods, cookies, and lemonades. I always toss a big hunk of ginger in my smoothies. To retain the most flavor and nutrients, it is best to add ginger at the end of cooking. The easiest way to use fresh ginger is to finely grate it, skin on, then place the grated ginger in your palm and squeeze the ginger juice into the dish and discard the pulp. Surprisingly, lots of flavorful juice will come out! Benefits: warms the body; has anti-inflammatory properties; improves circulation; aids in digestion; relieves gas, motion sickness, nausea, and menstrual cramps.

Grains

"Whole grains" refers to cereal grains like wheat, oats, and brown rice. Grains in their whole form contain three parts: the bran, the germ, and the endosperm. A grain in its whole state is most nutritious. In contrast, a refined grain has had the bran and germ removed to increase shelf life; all that remains is the endosperm. This leaves the carbs without the nutrients! The bran and germ hold most of the grain's valuable vitamins, minerals, and oils and all of its fiber, making the grain a nutrient-rich whole food. Whole grains still have their healthful natural oils. Natural oils can oxidize and go rancid quicker than people think. It is important, therefore, to note that whole grains like brown rice *do not keep as long as refined grains like white rice*. Whole grains should be stored in a tightly sealed container in the refrigerator and be used within six months. They do not last forever, as no real food should!

Greek Yogurt

Select plain full-fat yogurt, then you have a blank canvas that you can flavor yourself. To make it

vanilla yogurt, you can simply add a few drops of vanilla extract and honey, or make it fruit yogurt by adding a large spoonful of your favorite fruit preserves. Read the ingredients labels on flavored yogurts at the grocery store and notice that they are loaded with artificial flavoring, sugars, calories, and preservatives, and are expensive to boot! Why pay for that when you can make it better yourself? The creamy texture of Greek yogurt holds up well in dips, smoothies, and baked goods, and is a healthful substitute for sour cream, mayonnaise, or butter. Greek yogurt has almost double the protein of regular yogurt, and tends to be lower in carbs. Benefits: excellent source of protein; good source of probiotics, potassium, and calcium; promotes gut health; supports immune system function; filling.

Green Chiles

Green chiles have been fire roasted and peeled. They are mild and sometimes sweet. They are often used in Mexican and Southwestern cuisine. These canned chiles typically come chopped or diced, either will work in this book.

Herbs

Fresh herbs tend to go bad quickly, so it is smart to plan to use them at the beginning of the week. For leafy herbs like cilantro, dill, parsley, and basil, rinse them in cold water, pat them dry, and place them in a jar with an inch of water, like a little bouquet of flowers. Tuck the jar in a safe spot in the fridge so it doesn't get spilled. Store them properly, and they can last three to five days. Herbs with woody stems, like rosemary, mint, and thyme, don't need to be kept in water. To retain the most flavor and nutrients, it is best to add fresh herbs at the end of cooking (last 5 minutes). They are meant to be enjoyed raw, so tear them by hand, and add fresh sprigs of herbs to your salad greens for exciting enhanced flavor! If you want to substitute fresh herbs in place of dried herbs, double or triple the amount called for. Rule of Thumb: 1 portion of dried herbs is equivalent to 3 portions of fresh herbs. Once you have entered the world of cooking with fresh herbs, you will never want to go without them! Benefits: has detoxifying

qualities, which help rid the body of heavy metal accumulation; good source of vitamins; rich in antioxidants; has antifungal properties; aids in digestion; improves brain function.

Honey

Select honey that is local. In my opinion, honey is the best sweetener as it is natural and unprocessed. Honey is great drizzled on yogurt, added to tea, or used to sweeten baked goods. To gain the most medicinal benefits from honey, purchase varieties that are raw and local; they are available at health food stores. Benefits: has antibacterial properties, helpful for treating seasonal allergies, reduces cough and throat irritation.

Nuts

Select nuts that are unsalted and raw. Raw nuts are best as nutrients can be lost in the roasting process. Buy nuts in their whole form and chop them yourself to reduce their exposure to oxygen, which causes the natural fats to oxidize, diminishing their vitamin content, and giving them a "stale" or "off" taste. Store nuts properly in tightly sealed containers in a cool, dry place away from sunlight. Storing them in the refrigerator or freezer will keep them fresh longer. Benefits: excellent source of protein, good source of healthful fat, rich in antioxidants, good source of B vitamins and minerals, has anti-inflammatory properties, promotes heart health.

Oats

Old-fashioned oats aka rolled oats, have been steamed and rolled flat so they cook faster. The bran, germ, and endosperm are still intact, so oats qualify as a whole grain. Did you know that instant oats aka quick oats, are just old-fashioned oats that have been chopped up so they cook faster? Both types are used in this book, and I've found that they can be used quite interchangeably. You can buy old-fashioned oats and make them into instant oats by pulsing them with a hand blender or in a food processor until they resemble instant oats. Do not process them to the point that they become powder; that would be making oat flour! Benefits: high in fiber, good source of protein and iron, high in manganese, good source of B vitamins, lowers blood cholesterol, stabilizes blood sugar, reduces risk of cardiovascular disease.

Olive Oil

Select cold-pressed extra virgin varieties sold in dark tinted bottles instead of clear bottles. Exposure to light causes this delicate oil to oxidize and go rancid. Extra virgin olive oil has fragile nutrients that can be damaged by high heat. To avoid this damage and to maintain the gorgeous flavor of quality olive oil, drizzle it onto foods at the end of cooking, right before serving. Purchase olive oil in sizes you can use within 6 months. Do not store oil near heat, like in that cabinet over your stovetop! Even though that may seem convenient, it causes them to go rancid quicker. Benefits: good source of healthful fat, rich in antioxidants, has anti-inflammatory properties, promotes heart health.

Onions

There are generally four varieties of onions sold in grocery stores: yellow, sweet, white, and red. There are slight differences in flavor, texture, and color, but they can usually be substituted for one another. In an effort to keep it simple, throughout this book I state yellow onion or red onion. If you love onions, you might prefer yellow or white onions, which are strong in flavor. Or you can opt for an all-purpose sweet onion like Vidalia. There is a lot of onion chopping happening in this book. If chopping onions really bothers your eyes, I suggest that you buy sweet onions. They are milder and tend to be less irritating to the eyes than yellow or white onions. Benefits: good source of calcium and magnesium, has anti-inflammatory properties, regulates blood pressure, promotes heart health.

Pasta

There are over 400 types of pasta, made of different flours and shapes, all of which yield different textures, colors, and flavors. The variety of flours that is used and available today in the grocery store is impressive: artichoke, semolina, buckwheat, rice, corn, spelt, and quinoa. I suggest branching out and trying different brands to create some diversity in your kitchen and on your palate! There is no right or wrong, there is just preference! In this book, I suggest whole wheat pasta. But again, substitute as is right for you.

Pomegranate

Select pomegranates with thin tight skins. The seeds inside should be plump, a deep ruby color, and bursting with juice. It's hard to gauge good pomegranates until you open them; it is always a surprise. Sometimes they can be disappointingly dry and flavorless. Across many cultures, this exotic fruit is a symbol of fertility and prosperity. Pomegranates are grown in warm dry climates; the best time of year to buy them is September to December. Pomegranate seeds are great on top of yogurt for a snack, on a salad for sweet crunch, or as a garnish for meat. For instructions on extracting the seeds from a pomegranate, see page 70. Benefits: rich in antioxidants, regulates blood pressure, promotes heart health.

Prosciutto

"Prosciutto" is Italian for "ham" and refers to ham that has been cured and air-dried. It is sliced super thin, is very salty, and melts in your mouth. Prosciutto is a delicacy and one of the few "specialty" ingredients I ask you to buy. You need only a few precious slices as it is called for only once for a very special breakfast, Malia's En*lightened* "Eggs Benedict" (page 126).

Protein Powder

Select vanilla flavor because it is more versatile, and you can flavor it however you like. Add cocoa powder and you've got chocolate protein powder. The type of protein powder you use is your preference. Do your research; it might take trying a few. I prefer plant-based protein powders, like rice, pea, or hemp. A scoop of protein powder is a wise addition to a smoothie or a bowl of warm cereal as the protein keeps you full longer.

Quinoa

Of all the grains, quinoa is the most nutritious and is regarded as a super grain. Da Da Daaa! Technically, quinoa is not a grain; it is a seed. What makes quinoa so attractive is that it possesses all the essential amino acids, which make it a complete protein, similar to the complete protein supplied by meat, fish, eggs and poultry. It has a nutty taste, a light fluffy texture, and cooks faster than rice. It can be added to any dish, hot or cold, and can be substituted for almost any grain or pasta. It can be used in baking, warm cereals, cold salads, and pureed into soups and dips. The ways I utilize quinoa in this book are a mere fraction of its possibilities. Benefits: excellent source of protein and iron, rich in antioxidants, has anti-inflammatory properties, promotes heart health.

Raspberry Preserves or Jam

Select brands with the least amount of added sugar. The less sugar the better; eight grams per serving or less. These will most likely be labeled "reduced sugar," not to be confused with "sugar free." Products labeled "sugar free" are completely different. "Sugar free" means a chemical sweetener was used in place of sugar; this I avoid.

Safflower Oil

Select cold-pressed refined varieties. Safflower oil has a higher smoke point than olive oil and is less fragile; therefore, use safflower oil when cooking at high heat, as in frying or baking. Safflower oil can be used as a substitute in any recipe calling for canola or vegetable oil. Benefits: good source of healthful fat, excellent source of vitamin E, lowers blood cholesterol, promotes heart health.

Salmon Fillet

Select the best quality salmon fillets available, that are wild-caught or local (depending on your location). If you don't like salmon, feel free to substitute any fillet of white flakey fish, like halibut, haddock, flounder, sole, or tilapia in any of my recipes. Fresh steamed fish is a low-fat, protein-packed alternative to canned tuna or deli meats, which are highly processed and full of nitrates. Benefits: rich in omega-3s, excellent source of protein, good source of vitamin B12, promotes heart health.

Sardines

Canned sardines are great toppers for salads. No, they aren't anchovies, and, no, they don't have the heads on them. Give them a try; you will be greatly surprised how good they are. I love sardines because they belong to a sustainable fish population. Since they are small fish that feed mainly on plankton, they have a low mercury count. I pack them with me when I travel for a protein-filled snack on the go! In the United States, the names "sardine" and "herring" are sometimes used interchangeably as they are both in the herring family. Canned sardines come packed in water, oil, tomato sauce, and mustard sauce; you can also buy them smoked–your preference. Select those packed in olive oil to avoid subpar oils like soybean or canola. Drain off the liquid, and add the sardines to any salad. Benefits: rich in omega-3s, excellent source of protein, good source of vitamin B12, supports bone health.

Scallions aka Green Onions

Scallions are young green onions whose mild flavor is less overpowering than regular white onions. Scallions are essential in Mexican and Asian cooking. They are great in cold salads (think pasta or potato), in salsa, stir-fries, and on baked potatoes. They make pretty garnishes on chili or tacos. Slice off the fuzzy root end of the bulb, and use the white and light green parts. The white has the most intense flavor, which becomes milder as you get to the light green, which is better for garnish. Discard the dark green tops of the scallions as they are tough and don't have much flavor. Benefits: rich in antioxidants; good source of vitamin K; has antibacterial properties; high in flavonoids, which support the immune system.

Spaghetti Sauce

Determine the best quality by the first ingredient

listed; it should be tomatoes, not tomato puree. There should be 4 grams of sugar, not 9. It is preferable for no sugar to be listed on the ingredients label at all. Do the best you can.

Spaghetti Squash

Spaghetti squash are large, light-yellow oblong squash. They weigh three to five pounds and are typically sold by the pound. If it's your first time trying this squash, I suggest buying a 3-pound one first to see if you like it and can use it up. Cooked spaghetti squash has a completely different texture than other winter squash and can be scraped into light stringy shreds that resemble spaghetti, hence the name. The flavor is very mild, which makes it a great accompaniment to any dish because it will never take away from the main attraction. It is the perfect filler food, so pile it on your plate for a big satisfying meal. A cup of spaghetti squash is only about 40 calories; it's a nice low-carb substitute for pasta. Add it to oatmeal, a stir-fry, or top it with pesto or red sauce. Benefits: low in calories, high in fiber, good source of potassium and vitamin C, filling.

Spices and Dried Herbs

Spices and dried herbs add flavor and beautiful color to our dishes. I cannot imagine cooking without them. They can be expensive if you have to go out and buy a bunch of them at once. I considered the expense, so the spices and dried herbs you buy get used across multiple recipes throughout this book. Once you have them, you will be set for a while. You may be surprised to find that you already have many of them, so check your pantry. But spices and dried herbs don't last forever. Over time, they lose their potency, flavor, and healthful qualities, so it is good to keep them in rotation and use them up! As you will see in my recipes, I love food with a punch; I garnish my food with lots of spices and dried herbs. It also makes the food pretty, so load them on! Dried herbs should be crushed in your fingers when added to food to release their natural oils. Do not store spices near heat, like in that cabinet over your stovetop! Even

though that may seem convenient, the heat destroys the spices. I buy my spices in the bulk section at the health food store. They are fresher, more affordable, and I can buy them in the quantities I need to refill my own jars. With that being said, do not buy those massive restaurant-size jugs of spices from wholesale clubs. These will become flavorless dust before you even have the chance to use them up.

Sugar

I try not to consume refined sugar and use it minimally in this book. Whenever possible, naturally processed sweeteners like honey and maple syrup are always better choices. Brown sugar is white sugar mixed with molasses, which changes its shade and flavor; it is still sugar. Sugar taxes the liver and negatively affects kidney function, the nervous system, nutrient absorption, metabolism, hormones, sleep, and mood. This is why I encourage you to avoid brands that have sugar listed on the ingredients label. Find another brand, make it yourself, or go without it. Sugar is cheap and is being unnecessarily added to every processed food, even salty ones! It is sneakily being labeled under different names like sucrose, beet sugar, evaporated cane sugar, corn syrup, and brown rice syrup, to name a few. Sugar addiction is real. It appalls me that food producers are trying to get away with slipping it into food, especially food marketed towards children.

Summer Squash

The two most common summer squash varieties sold in stores and used in this book are dark green zucchini aka Italian squash and yellow straightneck squash aka yellow squash. Throughout this book, I refer to them as zucchini and summer squash. Select squash with brightly colored, unblemished skin, roughly six inches in length. They have a nutty flavor and are crunchy and delicious raw, chopped in salads or cut into sticks and dipped in sunflower butter. I like to slice zucchini into rounds and dip them into salsa in place of chips. They are extremely versatile and are a healthful filler to add to mac and cheese or chili–sneak those veggies in to make those dishes go

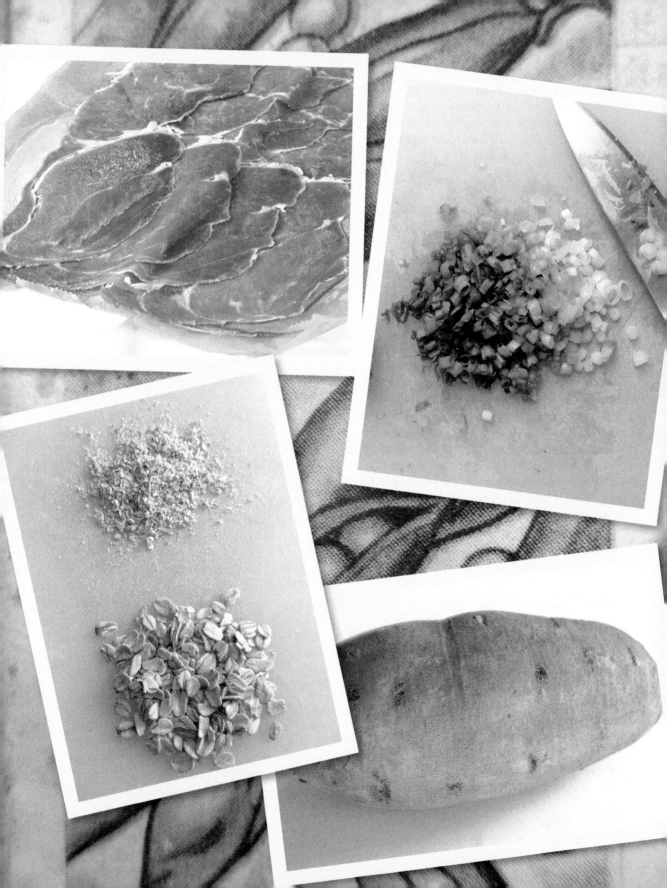

further. They cook quickly, so aim to undercook them to minimize nutrient loss. Benefits: good source of vitamin C, potassium, and magnesium; high in manganese, which helps the body effectively metabolize carbs and protein.

Sunflower Butter

Select brands without added sugar. Like tahini, it is made from seeds, and is, therefore, a good alternative for people with nut allergies. You can use it in place of peanut butter. It is great for snacks. On budget road trips, I keep a jar of this in my Purse Kitchen and dip veggie sticks, like carrots, celery, and zucchini in it. Don't knock it 'til you try it.

Sweet Potato

Select sweet potatoes that are firm and do not have any cracks or soft spots. I always select sweet potatoes that are similar in size, so that if I bake them, they will cook evenly. Store sweet potatoes in a cool dark place, away from heat. Sweet potatoes are packed with nutrients and have half the calories of white potatoes. They are delicious prepared savory or sweet. I always keep baked sweet potatoes in my fridge. I peel the skin like a banana and eat them cold with a hunk of coconut oil, usually while standing in my kitchen. Benefits: excellent source of carotenoids, rich in antioxidants, has anti-inflammatory properties, stabilizes blood sugar.

Tahini

International section. Tahini is a paste made from ground sesame seeds. Ingredients: 100% sesame seeds. It is often used in Greek, Turkish, Middle Eastern, and North African cuisine. Tahini is commonly known for being used in hummus. It is extremely versatile and can be made sweet in pastries, breads, and cookies, or savory in dips, dressings, and sauces.

Tuna

Select the best quality canned tuna that is pole caught, such as Wild Planet. It will be twice the price of most commercial brands, around $3.00 to $4.00 per can, but it's worth it. Select light tuna (skipjack or yellowfin) versus white tuna (albacore) as albacore tuna is found to have higher levels of mercury contamination. Due to the mercury levels found in albacore tuna the FDA recommends that women of childbearing age and children limit their consumption to no more than one can per week. Skipjack and yellowfin tunas are the most sustainable tuna populations as they reproduce quickly. Select tuna in water rather than oil to avoid subpar oils.

Turkey, Ground

Select the best quality ground turkey available. Look for words like "no hormones," "no antibiotics," "vegetarian-fed," "pasture-raised," "free-range," "local," and "95% lean." Ground turkey has great flavor and is a lighter option than beef. You can absolutely substitute ground beef for ground turkey if that is your preference, but give ground turkey a whirl–you might be pleasantly surprised! If you use beef, be sure to buy the best quality grass-fed, local ground beef you can get your paws on.

Vegetables

Choose vegetables that are deep in color. Think the more color, the more nutrients and antioxidants! Remember that size does not reflect quality. Bigger is not always better. For example buying the massive head of cauliflower over the medium one is only a good idea if you know you will use it. Keep in mind your intended use, so the vegetables will not go to waste. Use fresh vegetables within seven days. Once they start wilting, they are still edible, but they are losing nutrients fast! Cook them into a dish to keep them a little longer.

Worcestershire Sauce

Condiment section. Worcestershire sauce is a vinegar-based condiment that has flavors of tamarind, anchovies, soy sauce, onions, molasses, and garlic. It is the perfect combination of sweet, tart, and spicy–it will make your tongue dance. Worcestershire sauce adds boldness and depth of flavor to any dish. It is typically used to enhance the flavor in marinades, burgers, grilled meats, chili, or fried eggs.

Potato Salad Perfect

6 potatoes, cooked in jackets
   (4 cups, cubed)
1 onion, chopped
3 hard cooked eggs, sliced
1 cup chopped celery
1 cucumber, diced
1½ tsp. salt
¼ tsp. paprika
2 tblsp. vinegar   } or ¼ cp. Fr. Dr.
2 tblsp. French dressing
Mayonnaise

    Pour vinegar over
peeled potatoes while
still hot. Cool. Combine
all ingredients except
mayonnaise and marinate
in refrigerator for 1-6 hr.
   Just before serving
add mayonnaise and
mix carefully. If desired
add 1 tsp. celery seed
or 1 cup grated carrot

QUICK POTATO SALAD

4 cups cold, diced cooked potatoes
1 cup diced celery
½ cup sliced radishes
2½ tsp. Durkee's Onion Salt
½ tsp. Durkee's Ground Black Pepper

2 tsp. Durkee's Parsley Flakes
½ cup sour cream
¼ cup mayonnaise
1 tsp. cider vinegar

Put potatoes, celery, radishes in bowl. Sprinkle with seasonings. Combine sour cream, mayonnaise and vinegar and pour over the vegetables. Toss lightly. Makes 6 servings. Garnish with additional parsley flakes.

RESOURCES

Attenborough, Alison, and Jamie Kimm. *Williams-Sonoma Cooking for Friends: Fresh Ways to Entertain with Style.* N.p.: Oxmoor House, 2009. Print.

Balch, Phyllis A. and James F. Balch. *Prescription for Nutritional Healing: A Practical A-to-Z Guide to Drug-Free Remedies Using Vitamins, Minerals, Herbs & Food Supplements.* 3rd ed. New York: Avery, 2000. Print.

Brody, Jane E. *Jan Brody's Good Food Book: Living the High-Carbohydrate Way.* Bantam ed. Toronto: Bantam, 1987. Print.

Cox, Jeff. *The Organic Food Shopper's Guide.* Hoboken: John Wiley & Sons, 2008. Print.

Crowther, Lane, and Chuck Williams. *Fresh & Light* (Williams-Sonoma Lifestyles, Vol. 8) Alexandria: Time-Life, 1998. Print.

Fallon, Sally, and Mary G. Enig. *Nourishing Traditions: The Cookbook that Challenges Politically Correct Nutrition and the Diet Dictocrats.* 1999. Revised Second Edition. Washington, DC: NewTrends Publishing, Inc., 2001. Print.

Flinn, Kathleen. *The Kitchen Counter Cooking School: How a Few Simple Lessons Transformed Nine Culinary Novices into Fearless Home Cooks.* 2011. Reprint. New York: Penguin Books, 2012. Print.

Graimes, Nicola. *Cooking with Wholefoods: A Guide to Healthy Natural Ingredients, and How to Use Them with*

100 Delicious Recipes Shown in 250 Beautiful Photographs. London: Lorenz, 2008. Print.

Haas, Elson M. *The Staying Healthy Shopper's Guide: Feed Your Family Safely by Learning to Avoid: Additives, Preservatives, Pesticides, Pathogens, Processed Foods and More...* Berkeley: Celestial Arts, 1999. Print.

Herbst, Sharon Tyler, and Ron Herbst. *The Deluxe Food Lover's Companion.* Hauppauge: Barrons Educational Series, 2009. Print.

Jacobi, Dana. *The Essential Best Foods Cookbook: 225 Irresistible Recipes Featuring the Healthiest and Most Delicious Foods.* Emmaus: Rondale, 2008. Print.

Kelly, Melissa, and Eve Adamson. *Mediterranean Women Stay Slim Too: Eating to Be Sexy, Fit and Fabulous.* New York: Collins, 2006. Print.

Lagasse, Emeril. *Emeril's Potluck: Comfort Food with a Kicked-Up Attitude.* New York: William Marrow, 2004. Print.

Mateljan, George. *The World's Healthiest Foods: Essential Guide for the Healthiest Way of Eating.* Seattle: George Mateljan Foundation, 2007. Print.

Moore, Margaret, and Bob Tschannen-Moran. *Coaching Psychology Manual.* Philadelphia: Wolters Kluwer Health/Lippincott, Williams & Wilkins, 2010. Print.

Ostmann, Barbara Gibbs, and Jane L. Baker. *The Recipe*

Writer's Handbook. Hoboken: Wiley, 2001. Print.

Pollan, Michael. *Food Rules: An Eater's Manual.* New York: Penguin, 2009. Print.

Stuart, Tristram. "The Global Food Waste Scandal" TED. TEDSalon, London. May 2012. Lecture.

Waxman, Nach and Matt Sartwell. *The Chef Says: Quotes, Quips and Words of Wisdom.* New York: Princeton Architectural Press, 2014. Print.

Weinstein, Bruce, and Mark Scarbrough. *Cooking Know-How: Be a Better Cook with Hundreds of Easy Techniques, Step-by-Step Photos, and Ideas for Over 500 Great Meals.* Hoboken: John Wiley 7 Sons, 2009. Print.

Wood, Rebecca. *Quinoa the Supergrain: Ancient Food for Today.* New York: Japan Publications, 1989. Print.

On-line Articles and Websites

Donofrio, Liz. "Can Cursing Be Good for Your Health?" *ahchealthenews.com.* Advocate Health Care, 10 March 2014. Web. 10 November 2014. *ahchealthenews.com/ author/liz-donofrio*

Matheny, Monica. "The Ultimate Guide to Oats" *TheYummyLife.com.* 20 July 2013. Web. 13 March 2013. *theyummylife.com/Oats*

Parfitt, Julian, Mark Berthel, and Sarah Macnaughton. "Food Waste Within Food Supply Chains: Quantification and Potential for Change 2050." *Phil. Trans. R. Soc. B September 27, 2010. 365 1554 3065-3081; doi:10.1098/ rstb.2010.01261471-2970* (2010): n. pag. *Royal Society Publishing.* Web. 15 November 2014. *rstb. royalsocietypublishing.org/content/365/1554/3065.full*

Plumer, Brad. "How the U.S. manages to waste $165 billion in food each year." *WashingtonPost.com.* Wonkblog, 22 August 2012. Web. 15 November 2014. *washingtonpost. com/blogs/wonkblog/wp/2012/08/22/how-food-actually-gets-wasted-in-the-united-states*

Pollan, Michael. "Out of the Kitchen, Onto the Couch." *nytimes.com.* 29 July 2009. New York Times Magazine. Web. 11 November 2014. *nytimes.com/2009/08/02/ magazine/02cooking-t.html?pagewanted=all*

Wilson, Tracy V. "How Swearing Works" *HowStuffWorks. com.* 30 November 2005. Web. 10 November 2014. *people. howstuffworks.com/swearing.htm*

Quotations

Briggs, Dorothy, Corkille. Quoted in: Moore, Margaret, and Bob Tschannen-Moran. *Coaching Psychology Manual.* Philadelphia: Wolters Kluwer Health/Lippincott, Williams & Wilkins, 2010. Print.

Colicchio, Tom. Quoted in: Waxman, Nach and Matt Sartwell. *The Chef Says: Quotes, Quips and Words of Wisdom.* New York: Princeton Architectural Press, 2014. Print.

Pollan, Michael. "Out of the Kitchen, Onto the Couch" New York: New York Times Magazine, 2009. Web.

Stuart, Tristram. "The Global Food Waste Scandal" London: TEDSalon, 2012. Lecture.

Thorisson, Mimi. Quoted in: Muhlke, Christine. *"Mimi Thorisson's Picture-Perfect Dinner Party in France"* New York: Bon Appétit Magazine, 2013. Print.

Weinstein, Bruce, and Mark Scarbrough. *Cooking Know-How: Be a Better Cook with Hundreds of Easy Techniques, Step-by-Step Photos, and Ideas for Over 500 Great Meals.* Hoboken: John Wiley 7 Sons, 2009. Print.

GOOD READS

These books were serious game changers for me. Some advice I used, and some I didn't. I dedicated this book to the life-long journey of educating ourselves and trying out new things. Listen to how your body responds, and then stick to whatever works for you. Cheers to the discoveries ahead!

Eat Right 4 Your Type: The Individualized Diet Solution to Staying Healthy, Living Longer, & Achieving Your Ideal Weight. By Peter J. D'Adamo with Catherine Whitney

Food Rules: An Eater's Manual. By Michael Pollan (I recommend all of his books)

It Starts with Food: Discover the Whole30 and Change Your Life in Unexpected Ways. By Dallas and Melissa Hartwig

Kitchen Counter Cooking School: How a Few Simple Lessons Transformed Nine Culinary Novices into Fearless Home Cooks. By Kathleen Flinn

Nourishing Traditions: The Cookbook that Challenges Politically Correct Nutrition and the Diet Dictocrats. By Sally Fallon with Mary G. Enig, Ph.D.

The Essential Best Foods Cook Book: 225 Irresistible Recipes Featuring the Healthiest and Most Delicious Foods. By Dana Jacobi

The Staying Healthy Shopper's Guide: Feed Your Family Safely by Learning to Avoid: Additives, Preservatives, Pesticides, Pathogens, Processed Foods and More… By Elson M. Haas, M.D

The World's Healthiest Foods: Essential Guide for the Healthiest Way of Eating. By George Mateljan

Inspiring Documentaries

Food Inc. Directed by Robert Kenner. Released 2008

Forks Over Knives. Directed by Lee Fulkerson. Released 2011

Just Eat It. Directed by Grant Baldwin. Released 2014

INGREDIENT INDEX

RECIPE INDEX

CPSIA information can be obtained
at www.ICGtesting.com
Printed in the USA
LVOW05s0822290216

477120LV00041B/970/P